English Language Arts — Level **C**

Measuring Up®

to the

Common Core

PeoplesEducation.com

Peoples **E**ducation
Your partner in student success®

Chief Development Officer: Michael Urban

Vice President, Curriculum and Development: Elisa Eiger

Vice President of Sales and Marketing: Victoria Ameer Kiely

Associate Vice President of Marketing: Angela Glock

Director of Project Management: Lynne Naylor

Editorial Development: Words & Numbers, Publisher's Partnership

Editor: Joanne Willard

Copy Editor: Shelly Rawson

Development Services Controller: Jason Grasso

Director, Asset Management: Kristine Liebman

Development Services Assistant: Amy Priddy Wierzbicki

Manager, User Experience: Jennifer Tully

Senior Production Manager: Steven Genzano

Production: Planman Technologies

Cover Design: Joe Guerrero, Todd Kochakji

Acknowledgments:
p. 17, photograph, Copyright © iStockphoto
p. 122, illustration, Shutterstock.com, © Matthew Cole

Your partner in student success®

Copyright © 2013
Peoples Education, Inc.
299 Market Street
Saddle Brook, New Jersey 07663

ISBN 978-1-61526-920-4

Printed in the United States of America.

10   9   8   7   6   5

Table of Contents

Chapter 1   Foundational Skills

Chapter 2   Third-Grade Language Skills

Chapter 3   Reading Literature

Chapter 4   Reading Informational Texts

Chapter 5   Writing

Handbooks

Appendices

Your teacher may choose to assign practice tests for this program to check your learning.

Table of Reading Selections

Lesson	Reading Passage	Type				Curricular Connection	Word Count	Reading Level
		Fiction	Nonfiction	Literary	Informational			
1	Stargazing has been...		✓		✓	History	108	900
2	Jamal looked at...	✓		✓			62	630
3	Ian tried to...	✓		✓			116	770
4	Meet the Timberdoodle		✓		✓	Science	127	720
4	Help Is Coming		✓		✓	Science	117	630
5	Without hesitation, little...	✓		✓			30	660
5	"What would you like to see..."	✓		✓		History	123	550
6	Michelle was terrifed...	✓		✓		Sports	166	540
11	Ms. Ruiz's classroom...	✓		✓			177	520
12	The Magic Coin	✓		✓			93	590
12	A Wet Surprise	✓		✓			131	620
13	"The Hare and the Tortoise" by...		✓		✓	Literature	139	660
14	Jamal lay on the couch...	✓		✓			82	700
14	Tia for President!	✓		✓		Social Studies	139	550
15	Bird on the Loose	✓		✓			123	640
15	Danger on the Lake	✓		✓			138	690
16	from "Jack and the Beanstalk"	✓		✓		Literature	93	700
16	Rapunzel's Tower	✓		✓		Literature	133	590
17	'The Lion and the Mouse' by Aesop	✓		✓		Literature	121	670
17	The Lightning Bug and the Jackdaw	✓		✓		Multicultural	159	700
18	Mina's Overnight	✓		✓			167	740
18	The Dance Recital	✓		✓		Music/Arts	54	430
18	The Vain Jackdaw	✓		✓		Literature	81	900
18	The Peacock and the Crane	✓		✓		Literature	65	640
19	In the Well		✓	✓			114	580
19	Sudden Storm	✓		✓			172	670
20	Mountain Sunrise		✓	✓		Sports	104	630
20	Yumi's Tryout	✓		✓		Music/Arts	145	590
21	Prairie Dogs		✓		✓	History, Science	70	790
21	River otters are playful acrobats...		✓		✓	Science	49	760

Lesson	Reading Passage	Type				Curricular Connection	Word Count	Reading Level
		Fiction	Nonfiction	Literary	Informational			
22	Saving Sequoias		✓		✓	History	176	750
22	Saving Yosemite		✓		✓	History	60	980
23	Rachel Carson and *Silent Spring*		✓		✓	Science	183	780
24	Lewis and Clark		✓		✓	History	231	780
25	Caribou		✓		✓	History	71	760
26	Phases of the Moon		✓		✓	Science	113	790
27	Highways		✓		✓	Social Studies	83	760
27	Country Roads		✓		✓	Social Studies	81	830
28	The Cardinal		✓		✓	Science	115	710
28	Birds		✓		✓	Science	134	780

Correlation to the Common Core State Standards

Common Core State Standards	Lessons
College and Career Readiness Anchor Standards for Reading, Grades K-5	
Key Ideas and Details	
CCR.R.1 Read closely to determine what the text says explicitly and to make logical inferences from it; cite specific textual evidence when writing or speaking to support conclusions drawn from the text.	12, 22, KIU 3, 4
CCR.R.2 Determine central ideas or themes of a text and analyze their development; summarize the key supporting details and ideas.	13, 17, 21, 22, KIU 3, 4
CCR.R.3 Analyze how and why individuals, events, and ideas develop and interact over the course of a text.	14, 15, 24, KIU 3, 5
Craft and Structure	
CCR.R.4 Interpret words and phrases as they are used in a text, including determining technical, connotative, and figurative meanings, and analyze how specific word choices shape meaning or tone.	20, 28, KIU 1, 4
CCR.R.5 Analyze the structure of texts, including how specific sentences, paragraphs, and larger portions of the text (e.g., a section, chapter, scene, or stanza) relate to each other and the whole.	23, 24, KIU 4
CCR.R.6 Assess how point of view or purpose shapes the content and style of a text.	16, 25, KIU 4
Integration of Knowledge and Ideas	
CCR.R.7 Integrate and evaluate content presented in diverse media and formats, including visually and quantitatively, as well as in words.	19, 26, KIU 3, 4
CCR.R.8 Delineate and evaluate the argument and specific claims in a text, including the validity of the reasoning as well as the relevance and sufficiency of the evidence.	24, KIU 4
CCR.R.9 Analyze how two or more texts address similar themes or topics in order to build knowledge or to compare the approaches the authors take.	18, 27, KIU 3, 4
Range of Reading and Level of Text Complexity	
CCR.R.10 Read and comprehend complex literary and informational texts independently and proficiently.	4, 11, KIU 1, 3
Reading Standards for Literature, Grade 3	
Key Ideas and Details	
RL.3.1 Ask and answer questions to demonstrate understanding of a text, referring explicitly to the text as the basis for the answers.	12, KIU 3
RL.3.2 Recount stories, including fables, folktales, and myths from diverse cultures; determine the central message, lesson, or moral and explain how it is conveyed through key details in the text.	13, 17, KIU 3
RL.3.3 Describe characters in a story (e.g., their traits, motivations, or feelings) and explain how their actions contribute to the sequence of events.	14, 15, KIU 3

Key to Lesson References:

KIU = Kick It Up (numbered by chapter)
GUM = Grammar, Usage, and Mechanics Handbook (numbered by Mini-Lesson)
SLH = Speaking and Listening Handbook (numbered by Mini-Lesson)

Common Core State Standards	Lessons
Craft and Structure	
RL.3.4 Determine the meaning of words and phrases as they are used in a text, distinguishing literal from nonliteral language.	20, KIU 4
RL.3.5 Refer to parts of stories, dramas, and poems when writing or speaking about a text, using terms such as chapter, scene, and stanza; describe how each successive part builds on earlier sections.	11, KIU 3
RL.3.6 Distinguish their own point of view from that of the narrator or those of the characters.	16
Integration of Knowledge and Ideas	
RL.3.7 Explain how specific aspects of a text's illustrations contribute to what is conveyed by the words in a story (e.g., create mood, emphasize aspects of a character or setting).	19, KIU 3
RL.3.9 Compare and contrast the themes, settings, and plots of stories written by the same author about the same or similar characters (e.g., in books from a series).	18, KIU 3
Range of Reading and Level of Text Complexity	
RL.3.10 By the end of the year, read and comprehend literature, including stories, dramas, and poetry, at the high end of the grades 2–3 text complexity band independently and proficiently.	13, 17, 18, 19
Reading Standards for Informational Text, Grade 3	
Key Ideas and Details	
RI.3.1 Ask and answer questions to demonstrate understanding of a text, referring explicitly to the text as the basis for the answers.	22, KIU 4
RI.3.2 Determine the main idea of a text; recount the key details and explain how they support the main idea.	21, 22, KIU 4
RI.3.3 Describe the relationship between a series of historical events, scientific ideas or concepts, or steps in technical procedures in a text, using language that pertains to time, sequence, and cause/effect.	24
Craft and Structure	
RI.3.4 Determine the meaning of general academic and domain-specific words and phrases in a text relevant to a grade 3 topic or subject area.	28
RI.3.5 Use text features and search tools (e.g., key words, sidebars, hyperlinks) to locate information relevant to a given topic efficiently.	23, KIU 4
RI.3.6 Distinguish their own point of view from that of the author of a text.	25, KIU 4
Integration of Knowledge and Ideas	
RI.3.7 Use information gained from illustrations (e.g., maps, photographs) and the words in a text to demonstrate understanding of the text (e.g., where, when, why, and how key events occur).	26, KIU 4
RI.3.8 Describe the logical connection between particular sentences and paragraphs in a text (e.g., comparison, cause/effect, first/second/third in a sequence).	24, KIU 4
RI.3.9 Compare and contrast the most important points and key details presented in two texts on the same topic.	27, KIU 4

Common Core State Standards	Lessons
Range of Reading and Level of Text Complexity	
RI.3.10 By the end of the year, read and comprehend informational texts, including history/ social studies, science, and technical texts, at the high end of the grades 2–3 text complexity band independently and proficiently.	30
Reading Standards: Foundational Skills, Grade 3	
Phonics and Word Recognition	
RF.3.3 Know and apply grade-level phonics and word analysis skills in decoding words.	1, 2
a. Identify and know the meaning of the most common prefixes and derivational suffixes.	2, KIU 1
b. Decode words with common Latin suffixes.	2, KIU 1
c. Decode multi-syllable words.	1, KIU 1
d. Read grade-appropriate irregularly spelled words.	1, KIU 1
Fluency	
RF.3.4 Read with sufficient accuracy and fluency to support comprehension.	3, 4, 5
a. Read on-level text with purpose and understanding.	4, KIU 1
b. Read on-level prose and poetry orally with accuracy, appropriate rate, and expression on successive readings	5, KIU 1
c. Use context to confirm or self-correct word recognition and understanding, rereading as necessary.	3, KIU 1
College and Career Readiness Anchor Standards for Writing, Grades K-5	
Text Types and Purposes	
CCR.W.1 Write arguments to support claims in an analysis of substantive topics or texts, using valid reasoning and relevant and sufficient evidence.	29, KIU 5
CCR.W.2 Write informative/explanatory texts to examine and convey complex ideas and information clearly and accurately through the effective selection, organization, and analysis of content.	30, KIU 5
CCR.W.3 Write narratives to develop real or imagined experiences or events using effective technique, well-chosen details, and well-structured event sequences.	31, KIU 5
Production and Distribution of Writing	
CCR.W.4 Produce clear and coherent writing in which the development, organization, and style are appropriate to task, purpose, and audience.	KIU 5
CCR.W.5 Develop and strengthen writing as needed by planning, revising, editing, rewriting, or trying a new approach.	29, 30, KIU 5
CCR.W.6 Use technology, including the Internet, to produce and publish writing and to interact and collaborate with others.	29, 30, 31, KIU 5
Research to Build and Present Knowledge	
CCR.W.7 Conduct short as well as more sustained research projects based on focused questions, demonstrating understanding of the subject under investigation.	5, 29, KIU 5
CCR.W.8 Gather relevant information from multiple print and digital sources, assess the credibility and accuracy of each source, and integrate the information while avoiding plagiarism.	29, 30, KIU 5

Common Core State Standards	Lessons
CCR.W.9 Draw evidence from literary or informational texts to support analysis, reflection, and research.	12, 14, 15, 17, 18 21, 24, 27
Range of Writing	
CCR.W.10 Write routinely over extended time frames (time for research, reflection, and revision) and shorter time frames (a single sitting or a day or two) for a range of tasks, purposes, and audiences.	KIU 5
Writing Standards, Grade 3	
Text Types and Purposes	
W.3.1 Write opinion pieces on topics or texts, supporting a point of view with reasons.	29
a. Introduce the topic or text they are writing about, state an opinion, and create an organizational structure that lists reasons.	29
b. Provide reasons that support the opinion.	29
c. Use linking words and phrases (e.g., *because, therefore, since,* for example) to connect opinion and reasons.	29
d. Provide a concluding statement or section.	29
W.3.2 Write informative/explanatory texts to examine a topic and convey ideas and information clearly.	30, KIU 5
a. Introduce a topic and group related information together; include illustrations when useful to aiding comprehension.	30
b. Develop the topic with facts, definitions, and details.	30
c. Use linking words and phrases (e.g., *also, another, and, more, but*) to connect ideas within categories of information.	30
d. Provide a concluding statement or section.	30
W.3.3 Write narratives to develop real or imagined experiences or events using effective technique, descriptive details, and clear event sequences.	31, KIU 5
a. Establish a situation and introduce a narrator and/or characters; organize an event sequence that unfolds naturally.	31
b. Use dialogue and descriptions of actions, thoughts, and feelings to develop experiences and events or show the response of characters to situations.	31
c. Use temporal words and phrases to signal event order.	31
d. Provide a sense of closure.	31
Production and Distribution of Writing	
W.3.4 With guidance and support from adults, produce writing in which the development and organization are appropriate to task and purpose. (Grade-specific expectations for writing types are defined in standards 1–3 above.)	KIU 5
W.3.5 With guidance and support from peers and adults, develop and strengthen writing as needed by planning, revising, and editing. (Editing for conventions should demonstrate command of Language standards 1–3 up to and including grade 3.)	KIU 5
W.3.6 With guidance and support from adults, use technology to produce and publish writing (using keyboarding skills) as well as to interact and collaborate with others.	29, 30, KIU 5

Common Core State Standards	Lessons
Research to Build and Present Knowledge	
W.3.7 Conduct short research projects that build knowledge about a topic.	30, KIU 5
W.3.8 Recall information from experiences or gather information from print and digital sources; take brief notes on sources and sort evidence into provided categories.	29, KIU 5
Range of Writing	
W.3.10 Write routinely over extended time frames (time for research, reflection, and revision) and shorter time frames (a single sitting or a day or two) for a range of discipline-specific tasks, purposes, and audiences.	29, KIU 5
College and Career Readiness Anchor Standards for Speaking and Listening, Grades K–5	
Comprehension and Collaboration	
CCR.SL.1 Prepare for and participate effectively in a range of conversations and collaborations with diverse partners, building on others' ideas and expressing their own clearly and persuasively.	11, 12, 13, 14, 28
CCR.SL.2 Integrate and evaluate information presented in diverse media and formats, including visually, quantitatively, and orally.	SLH 2, 4
CCR.SL.3 Evaluate a speaker's point of view, reasoning, and use of evidence and rhetoric.	16, 25
Presentation of Knowledge and Ideas	
CCR.SL.4 Present information, findings, and supporting evidence such that listeners can follow the line of reasoning and the organization, development, and style are appropriate to task, purpose, and audience.	13
CCR.SL.5 Make strategic use of digital media and visual displays of data to express information and enhance understanding of presentations.	SLH 4
CCR.SL.6 Adapt speech to a variety of contexts and communicative tasks, demonstrating command of formal English when indicated or appropriate.	KIU 3
Speaking and Listening Standards, Grade 3	
Comprehension and Collaboration	
SL.3.1 Engage effectively in a range of collaborative discussions (one-on-one, in groups, and teacher-led) with diverse partners on grade 3 topics and texts, building on others' ideas and expressing their own clearly.	1, 4, 5, 24, 28, KIU 1, KIU 2, KIU 3, SLH 1
a. Come to discussions prepared, having read or studied required material; explicitly draw on that preparation and other information known about the topic to explore ideas under discussion.	1, 4, 5, 24, 28, KIU 1, SLH 1
b. Follow agreed-upon rules for discussions (e.g., gaining the floor in respectful ways, listening to others with care, speaking one at a time about the topics and texts under discussion).	1, 4, 5, 24, 28, SLH 3, 5
c. Ask questions to check understanding of information presented, stay on topic, and link their comments to the remarks of others.	1, 4, 5, 12, 24, 28, KIU 1, SLH 3, 5
d. Explain their own ideas and understanding in light of the discussion.	1, 4, 5, 24, 28, KIU 1, SLH 3
SL.3.2 Determine the main ideas and supporting details of a text read aloud or information presented in diverse media and formats, including visually, quantitatively, and orally.	KIU 3, SLH 2

Common Core State Standards	Lessons
SL.3.3 Ask and answer questions about information from a speaker, offering appropriate elaboration and detail.	4, SLH 2
Presentation of Knowledge and Ideas	
SL.3.4 Report on a topic or text, tell a story, or recount an experience with appropriate facts and relevant, descriptive details, speaking clearly at an understandable pace.	13, KIU 1, 2, 3, SLH 4
SL.3.5 Create engaging audio recordings of stories or poems that demonstrate fluid reading at an understandable pace; add visual displays when appropriate to emphasize or enhance certain facts or details.	KIU 1, 3, SLH 4
SL.3.6 Speak in complete sentences when appropriate to task and situation in order to provide requested detail or clarification. (See grade 3 Language standards 1 and 3 for specific expectations.)	KIU 2, SLH 3
College and Career Readiness Anchor Standards for Language	
Conventions of Standard English	
CCR.L.1 Demonstrate command of the conventions of standard English grammar and usage when writing or speaking.	GUM
CCR.L.2 Demonstrate command of the conventions of standard English capitalization, punctuation, and spelling when writing.	GUM
Knowledge of Language	
CCR.L.3 Apply knowledge of language to understand how language functions in different contexts, to make effective choices for meaning or style, and to comprehend more fully when reading or listening.	7, 8, 9
Vocabulary Acquisition and Use	
CCR.L.4 Determine or clarify the meaning of unknown and multiple-meaning words and phrases by using context clues, analyzing meaningful word parts, and consulting general and specialized reference materials, as appropriate.	2, 3, 6, 10
CCR.L.5 Demonstrate understanding of figurative language, word relationships, and nuances in word meanings.	7, 8, 9
CCR.L.6 Acquire and use accurately a range of general academic and domain-specific words and phrases sufficient for reading, writing, speaking, and listening at the college and career readiness level; demonstrate independence in gathering vocabulary knowledge when encountering an unknown term important to comprehension or expression.	2, 3, 6, 10
Language Standards, Grade 3	
Conventions of Standard English	
L.3.1 Demonstrate command of the conventions of standard English grammar and usage when writing or speaking.	GUM
a. Explain the function of nouns, pronouns, verbs, adjectives, and adverbs in general and their functions in particular sentences.	GUM 1, 4, 6, 10, 12
b. Form and use regular and irregular plural nouns.	GUM 3
c. Use abstract nouns.	GUM 2
d. Form and use regular and irregular verbs.	GUM 8
e. Form and use the simple (e.g., I walked; I walk; I will walk) verb tenses.	GUM 7
f. Ensure subject-verb and pronoun-antecedent agreement.	GUM 5, 9

Common Core State Standards	Lessons
g. Form and use comparative and superlative adjectives and adverbs, and choose between them depending on what is to be modified.	GUM 11, 13, 14
h. Use coordinating and subordinating conjunctions.	GUM 15
i. Produce simple, compound, and complex sentences.	GUM 16
L.3.2 Demonstrate command of the conventions of standard English capitalization, punctuation, and spelling when writing.	GUM
a. Capitalize appropriate words in titles.	GUM 17
b. Use commas in addresses.	GUM 18
c. Use commas and quotation marks in dialogue.	GUM 19
d. Form and use possessives.	GUM 20
e. Use conventional spelling for high-frequency and other studied words and for adding suffixes to base words (e.g., sitting, smiled, cries, happiness).	GUM 21
f. Use spelling patterns and generalizations (e.g., word families, position-based spellings, syllable patterns, ending rules, meaningful word parts) in writing words.	GUM 21
g. Consult reference materials, including beginning dictionaries, as needed to check and correct spellings.	GUM 21
Knowledge of Language	
L.3.3 Use knowledge of language and its conventions when writing, speaking, reading, or listening.	12, 28
a. Choose words and phrases for effect.	19, 20, 28, 30
b. Recognize and observe differences between the conventions of spoken and written standard English.	29, 30, 31
Vocabulary Acquisition and Use	
L.3.4 Determine or clarify the meaning of unknown and multiple-meaning word and phrases based on grade 3 reading and content, choosing flexibly from a range of strategies.	6, KIU 2
a. Use sentence-level context as a clue to the meaning of a word or phrase.	2, 3, KIU 1
b. Determine the meaning of the new word formed when a known affix is added to a known word (e.g., agreeable/disagreeable, comfortable/uncomfortable, care/careless, heat/preheat).	2, KIU 1
c. Use a known root word as a clue to the meaning of an unknown word with the same root (e.g., company, companion).	2, KIU 1
d. Use glossaries or beginning dictionaries, both print and digital, to determine or clarify the precise meaning of key words and phrases.	10, KIU 2
L.3.5 Demonstrate understanding of word relationships and nuances in word meanings.	7, 8, 9
a. Distinguish the literal and nonliteral meanings of words and phrases in context (e.g., take steps).	8, KIU 2
b. Identify real-life connections between words and their use (e.g., describe people who are friendly or helpful).	7, KIU 2
c. Distinguish shades of meaning among related words that describe states of mind or degrees of certainty (e.g., knew, believed, suspected, heard, wondered).	9
L.3.6 Acquire and use accurately grade-appropriate conversational, general academic, and domain-specific words and phrases, including those that signal spatial and temporal relationships (e.g., *After dinner that night we went looking for them*).	6, 7, 8, 9, 10

To the Student:

It's never too soon to prepare for your future. The same goes for learning the Common Core State Standards for your grade level. Learning these standards will help you succeed in your academic pursuits and prepare for college and your career.

The lessons in this book will help you learn all the Common Core State Standards for English Language Arts. This book is divided into five chapters. Each one focuses on a different set of skills that you need to read, write, speak, and listen critically. Each chapter matches one of the strands, or main categories, in the Common Core State Standards for English Language Arts:

- Reading Literature

- Reading Informational Text

- Reading: Foundational Skills

- Language

- Writing

Each chapter includes:

- A review of skills and key vocabulary

- Real-world examples

- Stories and nonfiction passages that stretch your thinking

- A variety of activities and questions that allow you to show your learning

- Practice with multiple-choice, short-answer, and extended-response questions

- Kick It Up activities that will boost your learning to the next level

Language and *Speaking and Listening* skills are woven into the reading and writing lessons. However, you'll also get a chance to focus on the standards that make up these two strands in the "Grammar, Usage, and Mechanics Handbook" and the "Speaking and Listening Handbook." The handbooks contain mini-lessons to help you build your communications skills.

The lessons in this book will help you build your English Language Arts skills and improve your thinking skills. The lessons may seem challenging at first, but keep at it and you will be a success!

Have a great school year!

Peoples Education
Your partner in student success®

to the
Common Core

To Parents and Families:

Peoples Education has created this book to help your child master the Common Core State Standards for English Language Arts. The Common Core State Standards, a set of K–12 grade-specific expectations that were developed by a consortium of states and coordinated by the National Governors Association and the Council of Chief State School Officers, define what it means for students to be college- and career-ready in the 21st century.

Each chapter in this book is focused on a different set of skills, matching the strands, or main categories, in the Common Core State Standards for English Language Arts:

- Reading Literature
- Reading Informational Text
- Reading: Foundational Skills
- Language
- Writing

Each chapter includes:

- A review of skills and key vocabulary
- Stories and/or nonfiction passages that stretch your child's thinking
- A variety of activities and questions that allow your child to show his or her skill comprehension
- Practice with writing prompts and multiple-choice, short-answer, and extended-response items
- Kick It Up activities to boost your child's learning to the next level

Language and *Speaking and Listening* skills are woven into the reading and writing lessons. In addition, a "Grammar, Usage, and Mechanics Handbook" and the "Speaking and Listening Handbook" contain mini-lessons to help build your child's communications skills.

For success in school and the real world, your child needs a solid English language arts foundation, and your involvement is crucial to that success. Here are some suggestions:

- Read aloud to your child. Find a quiet place to read. If the book has pictures, talk about them. As your child listens, ask him or her to anticipate what will happen next. Talk about the characters and what happens to them.
- Treat reading as a pleasure. Give books as presents and show that you like to receive them, too. Respect each other's private reading time.
- Take pride in your child's writing. Post it on the refrigerator. Keep a scrapbook. Write cards to family and friends together.
- As you listen to television or radio and watch movies, engage in a discussion about what you hear and see. Question information. Talk about how the information relates to your own experience. Ask for your child's reactions.

Get involved! Work with us this year to ensure your child's success. Reading, writing, speaking, listening, and language skills are essential both inside and outside of school. They will give pleasure throughout your child's life.

What's Inside: A Lesson Guide

Lessons in this worktext are divided into three sections in which the Common Core State Standards are introduced and explained, applied, and independently practiced.

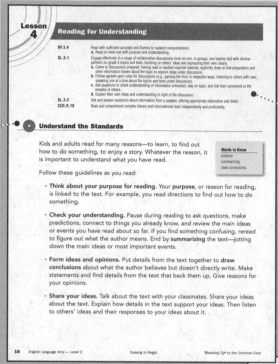

Understand the Standards introduces and explains the standards. The Words to Know box highlights important terms and vocabulary included in the lesson.

The Common Core State Standards on which the lesson focuses are clearly identified at the beginning of every lesson.

Guided Instruction features a reading selection with Guided Questions that help students apply the standards to the text. The guided reading selection may be followed by additional questions that challenge students to think about the text in deeper, more complex ways.

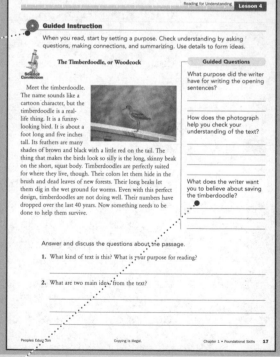

Guided Questions check comprehension and also help students think critically about the reading selection.

On Your Own

consists of items that challenge students to apply what they have learned and demonstrate their mastery of the standards.

3. What words does the author use to show how she feels about timberdoodles?

_____

On Your Own

Read the next part of the passage about timberdoodles. Record your reading process in the chart below. Share your ideas with a partner.

Help Is Coming

In 2001, a task force was formed to study timberdoodles. People wanted to find out why their numbers kept dropping. Scientists found out the main problem is loss of places they can live. Building causes some problems. Aging forests are a big problem. When forests get older, the brush these birds need disappears. They have no place to hide from animals that want to eat them. In 2007, the people on the task force made a plan to help. They will make more places that timberdoodles need: young forests. It seems odd, but to help the timberdoodle, trees need to be cut down and areas cleared. If all goes well, timberdoodle numbers should stop dropping by 2012.

Think about your purpose for reading. What kind of text is this? What is your purpose for reading?	
Check your understanding. What questions did you ask? What does this remind you of? What are the main ideas?	

4 What idea is mentioned in "Meet the Timberdoodle" that is explained in "Help Is Coming"?

_____

_____

5 **Elevate** On your own sheet of paper, write one of your opinions about the article or an idea in it. Discuss with a partner why you feel the way you do. Then share your opinions with a group of partners and then the class. Find the opinions you all can agree on.

6 **Critical Thinking** In a small group, investigate why some animals have become extinct in modern times. Some possible creatures are the dodo, the golden toad, the West African black rhinoceros, the Tecopa pupfish, and many others. Use books and the Internet to create your lists and gather information. Then divide the animals among members of the group. Discuss the reasons why they disappeared. Look for similarities and differences in the causes. Rank them in how severe you think the causes are. Share what you discover with the class in a multimedia presentation.

Icons make it easy to identify Elevate items, which require students to use higher-order critical thinking skills. Icons are also used to call out Critical Thinking exercises, opportunities for Collaborative Learning, and connections to media, school subjects, and real-world topics.

Kick It Up

At the end of each chapter, Kick It Up **project-based activities** provide a cumulative review of skills. Each Kick It Up activity is designed to challenge students with tasks that require deep thinking and skills such as research, collaboration, problem solving, using technology, and writing.

Make a Glossary

Are some words difficult for you to read? Do you have to stop each time you see a certain spelling pattern? A glossary of confusing words and spellings can help.

Work with a partner. Make a list of 10 confusing words or spelling patterns. Together, write a glossary entry for each word. After the word, write it the way it sounds. Write other words that have the same sound or spelling pattern. Use the word in a sentence with clues to the meaning.

Tough sounds like *tuff, rough, enough,* and *fluff.* The meat was so tough it was hard to chew.

Once you have written the entries, type them on the computer and print them out. Leave room after each entry to add visuals that help you remember the words. Use drawings of your own, photographs, or other images you download and print. Put your finished pages together in a booklet to share with the class. Keep a copy to look at as you read for school.

Build Words

Work in a group of four. Read the chart to make sure everyone knows the meanings of the prefixes, suffixes, and base words.

Prefix	Base Word	Suffix
dis-	trust	-able
re-	perfect	-er, -or
un-	teach	-ful
in-, im-	state	-ment

Divide into pairs. Work with your partner for five minutes to build as many words as you can from the word parts in the chart. When the time is up, meet with your group. Share your lists. Which pair has the most words? Put your lists together and share them with the class.

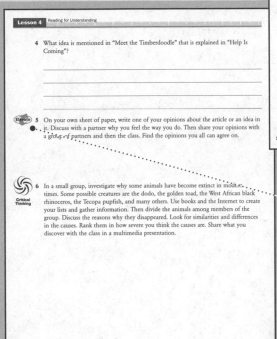

Lesson 1

Reviewing Phonics

RF.3.3	Know and apply grade-level phonics and word analysis skills in decoding words.
	c. Decode multisyllable words.
	d. Read grade-appropriate irregularly spelled words.
SL.3.1	Engage effectively in a range of collaborative discussions (one-on-one, in groups, and teacher-led) with diverse partners, building on others' ideas and expressing their own clearly.
	a. Come to discussions prepared, having read or studied required material; explicitly draw on that preparation and other information known about the topic to explore ideas under discussion.
	b. Follow agreed-upon rules for discussions (e.g., gaining the floor in respectful ways, listening to others with care, speaking one at a time about the topics and texts under discussion).
	c. Ask questions to check understanding of information presented, stay on topic, and link their comments to the remarks of others.
	d. Explain their own ideas and understanding in light of the discussion.

Understand the Standards

Science Connection

Imagine that you are reading your science textbook for homework. You come across this sentence:

> A constellation is a group of stars that makes up a certain pattern.

The word *constellation* may be new. Its meaning is given, but how do you say the word aloud? If you don't have a dictionary or glossary to check, sound out the word using the letters and syllables. You might know the word once you hear it.

Words are made up of letters. Letters stand for sounds. If you know the sounds letters stand for, you can put those sounds together to say the word. Words are made up of vowel sounds and consonant sounds. These sounds make up syllables.

> **Words to Know**
> vowels
> consonant
> syllables

- **Vowels** can be long or short. Vowel sounds are made by the letters *a, e, i, o, u,* and sometimes *y*. The *a* in *makes* is long. The *a* in *that* is short.

- **Consonant** sounds are made by letters that are not vowels. Some consonants can be hard or soft. The *c* in *constellation* is hard. The *c* in *certain* is soft.

- Some consonants work in pairs to make new sounds. The *t* and the *h* in *that* work together to make the /th/ sound.

- **Syllables** can be sounded out alone and then put back together to say the word. The word *constellation* has four syllables:
con • stel • la • tion.

Guided Instruction

Most of the time, spelling rules help you sound out words. But sometimes words do not follow the rules. These words you must look up, study, and memorize.

Example: The directions said to measure weight and height.

The rule is that *ei* stands for a long /e/ sound when it comes after a *c*. If it doesn't follow a *c*, it usually makes a long /a/ sound. This rule works to sound out *weight*. But *height* doesn't follow either rule. In this case the *ei* makes a long /i/ sound.

Answer and discuss these activities.

1. Read this sentence.

   The child discovered a pile of stones in the field.

   Which words have the long /i/ sound?

   _____ Pile _____

2. Say the word *shadow*. Does the *a* sound like the *a* in *class* or *danger*? Write two other words that have the same *a* sound.

   _____ class _____

3. Which word has the /sh/ sound that starts *shark—anchor*, *ancient*, or *mischief*?

   _____ shark _____

4. How many syllables does the word *possession* have?

   _____ 2 _____

5. Read this sentence.

   The difficult patient asked for a private room at the hospital.

   Which words in the sentence have two syllables? Three syllables?

   _____ difficult and hospital _____

6. What sound does *ei* make in *ceiling*? Is the *c* in *ceiling* hard or soft?

   _____ eel and hard _____

On Your Own

History
Connection

Read the passage. Then answer the questions with a partner.

Stargazing has been a popular hobby for thousands of years. Ancient astronomers looked at the stars and mapped patterns or pictures called constellations. The ancient Greeks and Romans used the stars to tell stories about their gods. For example, Sagittarius was placed in the night sky by Jupiter as a reward.

Some well-known constellations have multiple names. For example, Sagittarius is also known as the Archer. Ursa Major is known as the Big Dipper and is also sometimes called the Great Bear. The Little Dipper is another name for Ursa Minor, or the Small Bear. Even if you don't know the shapes and names of constellations, you can still enjoy gazing at the beautiful stars in the evening sky.

1 Circle the word that has the same vowel sound as *night*.

stargazing   ancient   pictures   (sky)

2 How many syllables make up *popular*? How should the word be divided?

2 and popular

3 Which words from the passage start with the same sound as *names*?

night

4 Which words in the first paragraph have the same number of syllables as *stargazing*?

popular

5 Which words in the passage have the same /e/ sound as *Greeks*?

evening

6 Which word has the same long /u/ sound as *drew*?

A beware

B found

C rustle

D suitcase

7 Which word does not have the same sound as the sound spelled by the letters *ou* in *bounce*?

   A ground

   B loud

   C nervous

   D mouse

8 How many syllables make up the word *ornament*? How should it be divided?

_____ 2 _____ ornament _____

 9 Read the sentence.

She read for hours last night in preparation for the test.

Which words have the same sound as the sound made by the *e* in *test*? What is another word with that sound?

_____ read _____

 10 When you read and find a word you don't know, you need to stop to figure it out. Discuss with a partner the steps you take to figure out how to say words you don't know. Then discuss your answer with another group of partners. Finally, discuss your answer with the entire class.

Critical Thinking

RF.3.3	Know and apply grade-level phonics and word analysis skills in decoding words.
	a. Identify and know the meaning of the most common prefixes and derivational suffixes.
	b. Decode words with common Latin suffixes.
L.3.4	Determine or clarify the meaning of unknown and multiple-meaning word and phrases based on grade 3 reading and content, choosing flexibly from a range of strategies.
	b. Determine the meaning of the new word formed when a known affix is added to a known word.
	c. Use a known root word as a clue to the meaning of an unknown word with the same root.
CCR.L.4	Determine or clarify the meaning of unknown and multiple-meaning words and phrases by using context clues, analyzing meaningful word parts, and consulting general and specialized reference materials, as appropriate.
CCR.L.6	Acquire and use accurately a range of general academic and domain-specific words and phrases sufficient for reading, writing, speaking, and listening at the college and career readiness level; demonstrate independence in gathering vocabulary knowledge when encountering an unknown term important to comprehension or expression.

Understand the Standards

Imagine you're reading a book. You see a word that looks familiar but you aren't sure what it means. Don't worry. It likely shares a word part with a word you already know. You can figure it out.

Words to Know
root word
prefix
suffix

You know *scarce* means "not enough." But what does *scarcity* mean? Break the word into parts to find out. This word is made up of *scarce* and *-ity*, which means "state of being." So, *scarcity* means "state of not having enough."

Words are made up of three major parts—prefixes, root words, and suffixes. Knowing the meanings of word parts can help you figure out new words.

○ A **root word** is a word's base. Root words give the words' basic meanings.

○ A **prefix** is a word part added to the beginning of a root word. Adding a prefix changes a word's meaning.

Word	Prefix	Meaning	New Word	Meaning
like	dis-	apart, not	dislike	to not like
appear	re-	again, back	reappear	show up again
known	un-	not, opposite	unknown	not known

○ A **suffix** is a word part added to the end of a root word. Adding a suffix changes a word's meaning. It can also change its part of speech.

Word	Suffix	Meaning	New Word	Meaning
love	-able (-ible)	able to, worthy of	lovable	worthy of love
act	-or (-er)	one who	actor	person who acts
excite	-ment	state or quality of	excitement	state of being excited

 ## Guided Instruction

When you see a word you don't know, break it into parts. First, look for the main part of the word. Think about words you know with that main part. Then, see if the word has a prefix or a suffix. Look at this list.

Prefix	Meaning	Suffix	Meaning
co-	together, with	-ful	full of
in-, im-	not, opposite	-less	without
pre-	before	-y	full of, made of, tending to

1. Which of these words have prefixes and which do not? How do you know?

comb	**insight**
copilot	**prepay**
inner	**pretty**

_____

_____

_____

 Measuring Up® to the Common Core

2. What words can you think of that end in *-ful*, *-less*, and *-y* that show the meaning of the suffix? How do you know the letters really are suffixes in those words?

_____

_____

_____

3. The word *possible* describes something that can be or can be done. What does the underlined word mean in the following sentence? Explain how you know.

Cleaning his room seemed like an <u>impossibility</u>.

_____

_____

_____

Read each sentence, and then answer the questions.

4. Jeannie's effort to finish the race was <u>respectable</u>.

What is the main word in *respectable*? What does it mean? What does *respectable* mean?

_____

_____

_____

5. Kara's mom told her to <u>preheat</u> the oven while she mixed the cake batter.

What two word parts make up *preheat*? What does *preheat* mean?

_____

_____

_____

6. **The frown on his face showed his <u>discouragement</u>.**

What is the main part of *discouragement*? What does it mean? What does *discouragement* mean?

_____

_____

_____

On Your Own

Read the passage. Use the chart to break apart the underlined words and tell their meanings.

Jamal looked at his <u>coworker</u>. He asked her to <u>reread</u> the instructions for putting together the bicycle. He knew it was <u>doable</u>. They were just having a hard time figuring it out. He didn't want to <u>displease</u> his boss and seem like a <u>careless</u> worker. When they started again, they were both <u>hopeful</u> that they would finish the bike without a problem.

Word	Prefix	Root Word	Suffix	Meaning
coworker				
reread				
doable				
displease				
careless				
hopeful				

Measuring Up® to the Common Core

Complete the following activities.

1 Which word shares a root with *unpack*?

A package

B untie

C wrapper

D undo

2 If you *agree* with someone, you share an opinion. What do you do if you *disagree*?

A You agree again.

B You do not agree.

C You agree before but not after.

D You agree with someone you work with.

3 Read the sentence.

The <u>dirty</u> dog ran through the house, leaving paw prints everywhere.

What is the root word of *dirty*? What does the word *dirty* mean?

_____

4 Divide the word *immovable* into three parts. What does each part mean? What does *immovable* mean?

_____

_____

5 Use what you know about prefixes, root words, and suffixes to figure out what each of these words means: *excitement, copilot, undependable, useful, player*. On your own sheet of paper, write the meaning of each word and use it in a sentence of your own.

RF.3.4	Read with sufficient accuracy and fluency to support comprehension.
	c. Use context to confirm or self-correct word recognition and understanding, rereading as necessary.
L.3.4	Determine or clarify the meaning of unknown and multiple-meaning word and phrases based on grade 3 reading and content, choosing flexibly from a range of strategies.
	a. Use sentence-level context as a clue to the meaning of a word or phrase.
CCR.L.4	Determine or clarify the meaning of unknown and multiple-meaning words and phrases by using context clues, analyzing meaningful word parts, and consulting general and specialized reference materials, as appropriate.
CCR.L.6	Acquire and use accurately a range of general academic and domain-specific words and phrases sufficient for reading, writing, speaking, and listening at the college and career readiness level; demonstrate independence in gathering vocabulary knowledge when encountering an unknown term important to comprehension or expression.

Understand the Standards

Imagine that you are reading a news article. You come across this sentence:

> People in the area talked about how convenient the new grocery store was, pointing out that it was open long hours and was no trouble to get to.

Words to Know

context clues

If you don't know what *convenient* means, you can use clues in the sentence to figure it out. What does the writer tell about the grocery store? It was open long hours and easy to reach. These examples are clues to the meaning of *convenient*. From the clues, you can figure out that *convenient* means "useful because it is easily reached and suited to a person's needs."

- **Context clues** are words and phrases in sentences and paragraphs that give hints to the meanings of other words. Context clues come in different forms. Here are some of the main kinds of context clues:

Definitions: The meaning of the word is written in the sentence.

> The locomotive, or <u>train engine</u>, was on <u>track 3</u>.

Examples: Details and descriptions give examples of a word's meaning.

> The nervous child <u>bit his fingernails</u> and <u>tapped his foot</u> as he waited to see the principal.

Restatements: A word's meaning is described using other, easier words.

> She used prior knowledge—that is, <u>what she already knew</u>—to help her answer the test questions.

Guided Instruction

When you read a word you don't know, reread the sentence to look for clues to its meaning. Look at the other words and phrases in the sentence to see how they work with the unknown word. Use these words to come up with a definition for the new word.

Example: The **professor** stood in front of the class and taught the college students how to write a report.

Find the Best Clues: "in front of the class"; "taught"; "college students"

Connect the Ideas: I know that teachers stand in front of the class and teach. The students are in college, so a professor must be a college teacher.

Try these examples yourself.

1. The salesman came to **demonstrate**, or show, how the sweeper worked.

   Find the Best Clues: _____

   Connect the Ideas: _____

   _____

2. Before choosing which coat to wear, Kari looked at the **thermometer** to find out how cold it was.

   Find the Best Clues: _____

   Connect the Ideas: _____

   _____

3. The teacher was not sure what kind of **transportation** the class would take to get to the museum—a van, a bus, or a train.

   Find the Best Clues: _____

   Connect the Ideas: _____

   _____

   _____

Read the passage and answer the questions.

Ian tried to pay attention but he just could not <u>concentrate</u> on the book he was reading. He was <u>bewildered</u> by the characters—he didn't understand why they acted the way they did. He put down his book and made a <u>decision</u>, or choice, to call his best friend, Joe. Joe wasn't home, so Ian called the new kid, Juan. Juan came over. They watched a <u>humorous</u> movie that made them laugh and laugh. Ian said they should make plans for the next week. They could watch another <u>ridiculous</u> movie that would be even sillier than the one they just watched. <u>Comical</u> Juan made a funny face, jumped up and down, and shouted, "Yes!" to the plan.

Guided Questions

What kind of context clue helps you figure out the meaning of the word *bewildered*?

_____

_____

_____

_____

What kind of context clue helps you figure out the meaning of the word *decision*?

_____

_____

_____

_____

What kind of context clue helps you figure out the meaning of the word *humorous*?

_____

_____

_____

_____

On Your Own

Collaborative Learning

Reread the passage in Guided Instruction and use context clues to find the meanings of the underlined words. Work with a partner to fill in the chart.

Word	Best Clues	Meaning
concentrate		
bewildered		
decision		
humorous		
ridiculous		
comical		

Read the sentence, then answer the question.

1 Michael confidently raised his hand because he was sure of the answer.

Which is the best clue to the meaning of *confidently*?

A raised

B hand

C because

D sure

2 Debbie searched for hours for the keys she misplaced.

What does *misplaced* mean?

A bought

B found

(C) lost

D needed

3 Gina will narrate the story of "The Three Little Pigs" for the kindergarten class.

Which words give the best clue to the meaning of *narrate*? What does *narrate* mean?

_____

4 The robber ransacked the house, dumping drawers and emptying closets to find money.

What does *ransacked* mean?

_____

 5 Read these sentences, then complete the activity.

My grandmother warned me not to become a spendthrift. She said it was important to save money and to spend it wisely when I needed something.

On your own sheet of paper, write the clues that help you figure out the meaning of *spendthrift*. Explain how you connected the clues to the meaning of the word.

RF.3.4	Read with sufficient accuracy and fluency to support comprehension.
	a. Read on-level text with purpose and understanding.
SL.3.1	Engage effectively in a range of collaborative discussions (one-on-one, in groups, and teacher led) with diverse partners on grade 3 topics and texts, building on others' ideas and expressing their own clearly.
	a. Come to discussions prepared, having read or studied required material; explicitly draw on that preparation and other information known about the topic to explore ideas under discussion.
	b. Follow agreed-upon rules for discussions (e.g., gaining the floor in respectful ways, listening to others with care, speaking one at a time about the topics and texts under discussion).
	c. Ask questions to check understanding of information presented, stay on topic, and link their comments to the remarks of others.
	d. Explain their own ideas and understanding in light of the discussion.
SL.3.3	Ask and answer questions about information from a speaker, offering appropriate elaboration and detail.
CCR.R.10	Read and comprehend complex literary and informational texts independently and proficiently.

 ## Understand the Standards

Kids and adults read for many reasons—to learn, to find out how to do something, to enjoy a story. Whatever the reason, it is important to understand what you have read.

Words to Know
purpose
summarizing
draw conclusions

Follow these guidelines as you read:

- **Think about your purpose for reading.** Your **purpose**, or reason for reading, is linked to the text. For example, you read directions to find out how to do something.

- **Check your understanding.** Pause during reading to ask questions, make predictions, connect to things you already know, and review the main ideas or events you have read about so far. If you find something confusing, reread to figure out what the author means. End by **summarizing** the text—jotting down the main ideas or most important events.

- **Form ideas and opinions.** Put details from the text together to **draw conclusions** about what the author believes but doesn't directly write. Make statements and find details from the text that back them up. Give reasons for your opinions.

- **Share your ideas.** Talk about the text with your classmates. Share your ideas about the text. Explain how details in the text support your ideas. Then listen to others' ideas and their responses to your ideas about it.

Guided Instruction

When you read, start by setting a purpose. Check understanding by asking questions, making connections, and summarizing. Use details to form ideas.

Science Connection

The Timberdoodle, or Woodcock

Meet the timberdoodle. The name sounds like a cartoon character, but the timberdoodle is a real-life thing. It is a funny-looking bird. It is about a foot long and five inches tall. Its feathers are many shades of brown and black with a little red on the tail. The thing that makes the birds look so silly is the long, skinny beak on the short, squat body. Timberdoodles are perfectly suited for where they live, though. Their colors let them hide in the brush and dead leaves of new forests. Their long beaks let them dig in the wet ground for worms. Even with this perfect design, timberdoodles are not doing well. Their numbers have dropped over the last 40 years. Now something needs to be done to help them survive.

Guided Questions

What purpose did the writer have for writing the opening sentences?

_____

_____

How does the photograph help you check your understanding of the text?

_____

_____

_____

_____

What does the writer want you to believe about saving the timberdoodle?

_____

_____

_____

Answer and discuss the questions about the passage.

1. What kind of text is this? What is your purpose for reading?

_____

2. What are two main ideas from the text?

_____

_____

_____

3. What words does the author use to show how she feels about timberdoodles?

_____

_____

On Your Own

Collaborative Learning

Read the next part of the passage about timberdoodles. Record your reading process in the chart below. Share your ideas with a partner.

Help Is Coming

In 2001, a task force was formed to study timberdoodles. People wanted to find out why their numbers kept dropping. Scientists found out the main problem is loss of places they can live. Building causes some problems. Aging forests are a big problem. When forests get older, the brush these birds need disappears. They have no place to hide from animals that want to eat them. In 2007, the people on the task force made a plan to help. They will make more places that timberdoodles need: young forests. It seems odd, but to help the timberdoodle, trees need to be cut down and areas cleared. If all goes well, timberdoodle numbers should stop dropping by 2012.

Think about your purpose for reading. What kind of text is this? What is your purpose for reading?	
Check your understanding. What questions did you ask? What does this remind you of? What are the main ideas?	

Form Ideas and Opinions. How does the author feel about the help for the timberdoodles? Which details tell how the author feels?	
Share Your Ideas. Share your ideas, reasons, and support from the text. Then listen to your partner. What reasons and support does he or she give for ideas?	

Complete these activities based on the passages in this lesson.

1   The most likely purpose for reading these passages is to

    A learn about timberdoodles.

    B be convinced to help timberdoodles.

    C enjoy a story about timberdoodles.

    D learn how to make new forest for timberdoodles.

2   Which question is not answered in the passages?

    A What do timberdoodles look like?

    B How many timberdoodles live in North America?

    C Why are numbers of timberdoodles dropping?

    D What are people doing to help timberdoodles?

3   List three questions that the author answers in these passages.

_____

_____

_____

4 What idea is mentioned in "Meet the Timberdoodle" that is explained in "Help Is Coming"?

_____

_____

_____

_____

 5 On your own sheet of paper, write one of your opinions about the article or an idea in it. Discuss with a partner why you feel the way you do. Then share your opinions with a group of partners and then the class. Find the opinions you all can agree on.

 6 In a small group, investigate why some animals have become extinct in modern times. Some possible creatures are the dodo, the golden toad, the West African black rhinoceros, the Tecopa pupfish, and many others. Use books and the Internet to create your lists and gather information. Then divide the animals among members of the group. Discuss the reasons why they disappeared. Look for similarities and differences in the causes. Rank them in how severe you think the causes are. Share what you discover with the class in a multimedia presentation.

Critical Thinking

RF.3.4.b	Read on-level prose and poetry orally with accuracy, appropriate rate, and expression on successive readings.
SL.3.1	Engage effectively in a range of collaborative discussions (one-on-one, in groups, and teacher led) with diverse partners on *grade 3 topics and texts*, building on others' ideas and expressing their own clearly.
	a. Come to discussions prepared, having read or studied required material; explicitly draw on that preparation and other information known about the topic to explore ideas under discussion.
	b. Follow agreed-upon rules for discussions (e.g., gaining the floor in respectful ways, listening to others with care, speaking one at a time about the topics and texts under discussion).
	c. Ask questions to check understanding of information presented, stay on topic, and link their comments to the remarks of others.
	d. Explain their own ideas and understanding in light of the discussion.
CCR.W.7	Conduct short as well as more sustained research projects based on focused questions, demonstrating understanding of the subject under investigation.

Understand the Standards

Real World Connection

Imagine reading aloud in class. You come across this sentence:

> "Can we *please* visit the aquarium next?" Judy begged.

Words to Know

rate

pronounce

expression

You might wonder why *please* is slanted or how to say "aquarium." The more you read aloud, the more natural you sound and the more interesting you make the reading for listeners.

Follow these guidelines to read aloud smoothly and easily:

- **Set your rate.** Your reading **rate** is the speed at which you read. Reading too quickly will likely cause you to stumble over words. Reading too slowly will sound choppy. Read at a comfortable rate that sounds like speaking.

- **Sound out words.** Skim a text before you read aloud. Find words you don't know how to **pronounce,** or say. Sound them out. As you read, take time to sound out words you stumble over. Connect letters to sounds, break words into parts, and sound them out. Often you will know words once you hear them.

- **Read with expression.** Show the feeling of a text with your voice. Look for clues for how to read. In the example above, the slanted *please* tells that the word should be emphasized. The word *begged* gives a clue about how to read the character's words.

- **Practice, practice, practice.** The more times you read a text, the better you will read it aloud. Practice reading several times to read smoothly and easily.

🌀 Guided Instruction

Prepare to read this text aloud. Skim it to find words that you don't know and sound them out to begin. Look for clues that tell how to read characters' words.

Without hesitation, little Jorge ran into the party and confidently announced, "I'm here! Let's play!"

All the children chuckled at his entrance and then invited him to join their games.

Guided Questions

Was your reading rate fast or slow the first time you read the text? Why?

_____

_____

_____

Answer these questions about reading the text aloud.

1. Skim the text. Which words do you need to sound out before you read aloud?

_____

2. Which words give clues about how to read Jorge's words?

_____

3. What word describes the feeling of this text—*scary, cheerful,* or *sad*? How can you read to show this feeling?

_____

_____

_____

Collaborative Learning

4. Take turns reading the text aloud with a partner. Read it at least two times each. Which words gave you trouble? How does the reading change the second time?

_____

_____

On Your Own

Prepare to read the passage aloud. Then take turns reading aloud with a partner.

"What would you like to see next?" Mrs. Ramirez asked Julia and her friends. They had already spent an hour in the Metropolitan Museum. The girls loved the ancient Greek and Roman statues. The African jewelry was also a big hit.

"Let's look at the armor next!" Julia excitedly suggested. "I love imagining what the people were like who wore it." The group of girls followed eagerly.

"This guy was *short*," Amanda giggled, and all the girls laughed as she pointed to a suit of armor that was about five feet tall. "This one wasn't at all," she noted, pointing at a huge suit.

The girls made up stories about the knights who wore the armor. Then they went to see the mummies.

Discuss and complete the following activities.

1 How did you read Julia's words? Which word gives a clue about how to read them?

_____

_____

2 What did you do when you found a word you could not pronounce?

_____

_____

3 What feeling did you try to express with your reading? How did you express it?

_____

_____

4 Which word has the same sound as the *ee* in *Greek*?

    A excitedly

    B people

    C laughed

    D went

5 This story is meant to be

    A boring.

    B scary.

    C fun.

    D serious.

6 Imagine you don't know how to pronounce the word *eagerly*. How would you break it down to sound it out?

_____

_____

_____

7 How did your reading rate change during the story?

_____

_____

_____

Elevate **8** Imagine you were directing a play of this story. On a separate sheet of paper, write instructions for the narrator, Mrs. Ramirez, Julia, and Amanda. Use clues from the text to tell each actor how to read his or her lines.

Make a Glossary

Are some words difficult for you to read? Do you have to stop each time you see a certain spelling pattern? A glossary of confusing words and spellings can help.

Work with a partner. Make a list of 10 confusing words or spelling patterns. Together, write a glossary entry for each word. After the word, write it the way it sounds. Write other words that have the same sound or spelling pattern. Use the word in a sentence with clues to the meaning.

Tough sounds like *tuff, rough, enough,* and *fluff.* The meat was so tough it was hard to chew.

Once you have written the entries, type them on the computer and print them out. Leave room after each entry to add visuals that help you remember the words. Use drawings of your own, photographs, or other images you download and print. Put your finished pages together in a booklet to share with the class. Keep a copy to look at as you read for school.

Build Words

Work in a group of four. Read the chart to make sure everyone knows the meanings of the prefixes, suffixes, and base words.

Prefix	Base Word	Suffix
dis-	trust	-able
re-	perfect	-er, -or
un-	teach	-ful
in-, im-	state	-ment

Divide into pairs. Work with your partner for five minutes to build as many words as you can from the word parts in the chart. When the time is up, meet with your group. Share your lists. Which pair has the most words? Put your lists together and share them with the class.

Learn Life Lessons

You can learn a lot about life by reading stories. Many stories share a lesson. You can learn the same things the characters do by thinking about what happens and how they handle problems.

Work in a small group. Each group member should choose his or her favorite story. Read your story. Discuss and answer these questions:

- What happens to the main character?

- How does the main character change?

- What lesson does the main character learn?

Meet with your group to share your answers. Work together to make a poster called "Lessons for Living." Choose the best way to write each story's lesson. Include descriptions, drawings, or photographs of times that the lesson might be useful. Hang your poster in the classroom.

Perform Poetry

Work with a small group to plan a poetry reading. Visit the library to explore books of poems. Each group member should choose a poem. Discuss as a group the best way to present each poem. Think about these ideas:

- What can I do with my voice to make it interesting?

- Should I play music as I read?

- Will showing pictures or drawings add to the poem?

- Should I show a video behind me?

After you decide how you will present your poem, practice with a partner. If possible, audiotape or videotape each other so you can decide for yourself what works and what doesn't. Then, practice your poetry reading as a group. Finally, put on your poetry reading for your class.

Lesson 6

Multiple-Meaning Words

L.3.4	Determine or clarify the meaning of unknown and multiple-meaning words and phrases based on grade 3 reading and content, choosing flexibly from a range of strategies.
L.3.6	Acquire and use accurately grade-appropriate conversational, general academic, and domain-specific words and phrases, including those that signal spatial and temporal relationships.
CCR.L.4	Determine or clarify the meaning of unknown and multiple-meaning words and phrases by using context clues, analyzing meaningful word parts, and consulting general and specialized reference materials, as appropriate.
CCR.L.6	Acquire and use accurately a range of general academic and domain-specific words and phrases sufficient for reading, writing, speaking, and listening at the college and career readiness level; demonstrate independence in gathering vocabulary knowledge when encountering an unknown term important to comprehension or expression.

 Understand the Standards

Real World Connection

Imagine that you are reading a story for class. You come across this sentence:

> **Words to Know**
> multiple-meaning word

> Harry and Sally realized they were in a jam, so they asked a friend for help.

If you don't know that the word *jam* has two different meanings, the sentence could sound pretty silly. "The people were in a fruit spread?" you might think. *Jam* is a multiple-meaning word.

- A **multiple-meaning word** is a word that has different meanings depending on the context in which it is used.

The word *jam* can mean "a spread made with fruit and sugar" or "a difficult situation."

English has many words that have two or more meanings. Sometimes the same word is used as different parts of speech. For example, a word might be both a noun and a verb.

In the sentence from the story, Harry and Sally ask for help to get out of a jam. The context clues tell you that the meaning of *jam* in this sentence is "difficult situation."

Guided Instruction

You will often come across multiple-meaning words when you read. If you are unsure of a word's meaning, you can use a dictionary, which will list all the different meanings of a word. You can use context clues (hints in the text) to figure out which meaning is correct for the sentence.

Sports Connection

Read the passage. Work with a partner to fill in the chart. Use a dictionary to write two meanings for each underlined multiple-meaning word. Then tell the meaning that fits the context of the sentence.

Michelle was terrified about playing in her first baseball <u>game</u>. Shaking, she peered out from the field and <u>saw</u> her mother and father. They were sitting together, wearing baseball caps with her team's logo, in the second <u>row</u> of the stands.

Michelle was the first one to <u>bat</u>. She looked anxiously at the pitcher from the other team and waited for her to throw the <u>ball</u>. The pitcher threw the ball <u>fast</u>. Michelle aimed her bat at the ball, closed her eyes, and took a <u>swing</u>.

"Strike!" called the umpire.

Michelle was so scared she wanted to go home. She looked out to see her mother <u>wave</u> from the stand. She took a breath, raised her bat again, and waited for the next <u>pitch</u>.

The ball came at her fast. This time, she hit it hard and sped to first base, where she slid in the mud.

She sighed in relief. She was <u>safe</u>. She waved back at her parents. She was glad they had come.

Guided Questions

When you find the underlined words in the dictionary, which meaning should you look for first?

_____

_____

How can context help you pick the other meaning?

_____

_____

_____

How can I tell the different meanings in the dictionary apart?

_____

_____

_____

Multiple-Meaning Words	Meaning
1. game	
2. saw	
3. row	

4. bat	
5. ball	
6. fast	
7. swing	
8. wave	
9. pitch	
10. safe	

 On Your Own

Choose the correct meaning of the word in the sentence. Explain your answer.

1 The man looked for water in the <u>well</u>.
Meanings: "fine," "hole in the ground that holds water"

_____

_____

_____

2 My bedroom is on the second <u>story</u> of the house.
Meanings: "tale," "level of a building"

_____

_____

3 I turned on the <u>light</u> so I could see.
Meanings: "pale," "lamp"

_____

_____

Complete the activities below.

4 Read the sentence below.

My mother paid the check at the restaurant.

Which meaning of *check* fits this sentence?

A test

B bill

C mark

D make sure

5 Read the sentence below.

They light the candle at night.

Which sentence uses *light* in the same way as the sentence above?

A Turn on the light.

B I put a light on the table.

C The dress is light blue.

D The campers light a fire to keep warm.

6 Write two sentences that use the word *row* to mean a) a fight and b) a line of people.

_____

7 Read the sentence below.

I saw a *bat* fly under a bridge.

Write another sentence that uses *bat* in the same way. Then write a sentence that uses *bat* in a different way.

_____

 8 If you come across a multiple-meaning word in a sentence, how can you figure out the meaning of the word?

L.3.5	Demonstrate understanding of word relationships and nuances in word meanings. **b.** Identify real-life connections between words and their use.
L.3.6	Acquire and use accurately grade-appropriate conversational, general academic, and domain-specific words and phrases, including those that signal spatial and temporal relationships.
CCR.L.3	Apply knowledge of language to understand how language functions in different contexts, to make effective choices for meaning or style, and to comprehend more fully when reading or listening.
CCR.L.5	Demonstrate understanding of figurative language, word relationships, and nuances in word meanings.

Understand the Standards

Science Connection

Say you come across this passage in a social studies class:

> Albert Einstein was curious about the world. He studied hard to learn more about physics, a type of science. He did experiments to figure out how to solve difficult problems.

You can make connections between words you read and their use in **real-life** situations. Think about the word *curious*. The passage tells you that Einstein was curious and gives examples of how he was curious: He studied and he did experiments because he wanted to learn.

Think about a person you know who is curious. How does this person act? Perhaps your little sister is curious. She might ask a lot of questions. Maybe she often wants to learn something new. Making this real-life connection between a word and what you know will help you understand the people and things that you read about.

Words to Know

real-life

Guided Instruction

Read the word and its definition. Then, connect it to real life to show that you understand what it means.

> **Example:**
>
> **disappointed:** upset and let down
>
> **Connect to real life:** It rained the day of my picnic. I was very disappointed. I cried and I slept for two hours. Being disappointed is hard!

Try these examples yourself.

1. **enormous:** really big

   Connect to real life: _____

   _____

   _____

   _____

2. **helpful:** ready to be useful

   Connect to real life: _____

   _____

   _____

   _____

3. **excited:** eager, can't wait

   Connect to real life: _____

   _____

   _____

   _____

 Measuring Up® to the Common Core

On Your Own

Discuss In a small group, read each sentence. Connect the underlined word to real life. Then think about how what you know can help you understand the sentence.

Example:

Read: The man was upset because the workers he hired were <u>careless</u>.

Connect to real life: My older brother is careless. He always leaves his toys in the hallway and trips over things because he isn't paying attention.

Think about the sentence: If I think about what my careless brother does, I can guess the workers didn't do a very good job.

Try these examples yourself.

1 **Read:** The boss was very <u>grateful</u> that the worker stayed late. So she gave the worker a raise.

   Connect to real life: _____

   _____

   _____

   Think about the sentence: _____

   _____

   _____

2 **Read the sentence:** The new student is <u>friendly</u>.

   Connect to real life: _____

   _____

   _____

   Think about the sentence: _____

   _____

   _____

3 Read the sentence: The family was so happy about their <u>playful</u> puppy.

Connect to real life: _____

_____

_____

Think about the sentence: _____

_____

_____

Complete the following.

4 A <u>cruel</u> person would most likely

    A give a gift.

    B say something mean.

    C help a friend.

    D shake someone's hand.

5 Read the sentences below.

> **The boy's cheeks were red. He lowered his head. He was sad he had stolen the candy. He was very upset that Mr. Brown had caught him.**

Think about this real-life example. What word best describes the boy?

    A curious

    B useful

    C alone

    D ashamed

6 Think about a time when you were <u>careful</u>. What did you do?

_____

_____

7 Read the sentence below.

The boys were jealous that the girls swam first.

Tell one thing the boys might do because they are jealous. Think about your own life.

_____

_____

_____

_____

8 Read these sentences.

The young girl was very impatient. She wanted her new doll now! She went to find her mother.

Think about a time when you were impatient. What did you do or feel? Then think about the girl in the sentences. What can you tell about her after thinking about your life? Write your answer on a separate sheet of paper.

L.3.5	Demonstrate understanding of word relationships and nuances in word meanings. **a.** Distinguish the literal and nonliteral meanings of words and phrases in context.
L.3.6	Acquire and use accurately grade-appropriate conversational, general academic, and domain-specific words and phrases, including those that signal spatial and temporal relationships.
CCR.L.3	Apply knowledge of language to understand how language functions in different contexts, to make effective choices for meaning or style, and to comprehend more fully when reading or listening.
CCR.L.5	Demonstrate understanding of figurative language, word relationships, and nuances in word meanings.

Understand the Standards

Language Connection

You come across this passage in your reading.

> My friend Louis swept me off my feet when I heard him play the violin. I could not make up my mind about still playing. He was so much better than I was. Mom told me to take a step back and decide later.

Words to Know

literal meaning

nonliteral (figurative) meaning

context clues

This passage contains words that are used in unusual ways. For example, did Louis actually knock the writer over? How does a person "make up her mind"? Does the mother *really* want the writer to "take a step back"? How would that help?

Writers use words in ways that are not always straightforward. Knowing figurative meanings of words and phrases can help you read and listen with better understanding.

- **Literal meanings** are dictionary meanings:
  - "To sweep" literally means "to brush" or "to clean."
  - "To take a step back" literally means "to move backward."

- **Nonliteral, or figurative, meanings** cannot be guessed by looking at the definitions of the words in the phrase.
  - "To sweep off one's feet" means "to impress."
  - "To make up one's mind" means "to decide."
  - "To take a step back" means "to stop and think."

You can use **context clues**, words or phrases in the passage, to help you guess the meaning of words or phrases you don't know.

Guided Instruction

Read the sentences. Write the word or words (context clues) that help you guess the meaning of the word. Then circle the meaning that best fits the sentence.

Example: The kids were giggling and making funny faces. Their mom told them not to <u>horse around</u>.

Context Clues: giggling, making funny faces

Meaning: ride a horse   fall over   (be silly)

Try these examples yourself.

1. **Example:** The teacher got impatient. He said, "<u>Step on the gas</u>, kids. We're going to be late!"

   Context Clues: _____

   Meaning: fall on a slippery spot   hurry   drive a car

2. **Example:** Everyone went to play except Sally. She had a broken leg and stayed behind. She told us later we had <u>left her out in the cold</u>.

   Context Clues: _____

   Meaning: made her stay outside   gave her a cold   did not include her

3. **Example:** I was nervous about singing in the play, but my teacher said, "Do not <u>lose sleep over it</u>. You will do great."

   Context Clues: _____

   Meaning: worry   get tired   sing

On Your Own

Discuss

In a small group, read the sentences. Write context clues that help you figure out what the nonliteral phrases mean. Then write a definition in your own words.

Example: Jan tried not to get mad at her puppy. However, when the puppy ate her shoes, Jan <u>lost her temper.</u>

Context Clues: get mad at, ate her shoes

Meaning: got angry

Try these examples yourself.

1 Read the sentence: We used a map, but we still <u>lost our way</u>. We took the wrong road and had to turn around.

Find the context clues: _____

Write the meaning: _____

2 Read the sentence: The girl was wriggling and running around while her mother tried to tie a bow in her hair. Her mother told her, "<u>Hold still</u>!"

Find the context clues: _____

Write the meaning: _____

3 Read the sentence: Every day, the boy looked at the new red bicycle at the store. He <u>had an itch</u> to ask if he could take it for a ride. He thought it would be so much fun.

Find the context clues: _____

Write the meaning: _____

Complete these activities.

4 Read the sentence below.

The student knew she was <u>in hot water</u> when she forgot her homework.

What does the phrase "in hot water" mean?

A in a bath

B in trouble

C feeling sick

D dirty

5 Read the sentence below.

My friends <u>drop by</u> all the time. My father says they should ask before they visit.

Which word is a context clue that helps you guess the meaning of "drop by"?

A time

B father

C ask

D visit

6 Read this sentence.

When the rain started, we had to <u>drop everything</u> and go inside.

What is the literal meaning of "drop everything"? What do you think is the nonliteral meaning of the phrase "drop everything"?

_____

_____

_____

7 Read the sentence below.

The children <u>made believe</u> they were kings and queens in a magic garden.

Tell which words help you guess the meaning of "made believe." Then write your own definition of the words.

_____

_____

Writing Connection

8 Tell what you know about nonliteral phrases. Give an example of a nonliteral phrase and tell what it means. Explain how they are different from literal phrases. Write your answer on a separate sheet of paper.

Measuring Up® to the Common Core

L.3.5	Demonstrate understanding of word relationships and nuances in word meanings. **c.** Distinguish shades of meaning among related words that describe states of mind or degrees of certainty.
L.3.6	Acquire and use accurately grade-appropriate conversational, general academic, and domain-specific words and phrases, including those that signal spatial and temporal relationships.
CCR.L.3	Apply knowledge of language to understand how language functions in different contexts, to make effective choices for meaning or style, and to comprehend more fully when reading or listening.
CCR.L.5	Demonstrate understanding of figurative language, word relationships, and nuances in word meanings.

Understand the Standards

Perhaps you overhear a conversation between two friends.

"Are you willing to see this movie, even though we have not read a review?" Philip asks.

"Yes. I'm keen to see it!" replies James.

As these boys talk, they use words with similar meanings: *willing* and *keen*. However, even though the words are similar, they have slightly different meanings. Learning how words' meanings differ slightly will help you understand what you read and hear.

Shades of meaning refer to the slightly different meanings similar words have.

- *Willing* means "ready to do something without being forced."

- *Keen* means "very eager and willing."

So in the conversation above, Philip asks James if he is okay with going to the movie, and James uses the word *keen* to show that he is actually excited about going.

You can use a dictionary or a thesaurus, as well as context clues, to help you determine shades of meaning as you read.

Guided Instruction

Read the pairs of sentences. Then answer the questions that follow each pair.

Example: Kate is <u>scared</u> of the dentist. Jim is <u>terrified</u> of the dentist.

Who is more afraid of the dentist? How do you know?

Jim is more afraid. *Terrified* means "extremely scared."

Try these examples yourself.

1. The little boys were <u>overjoyed</u> by the party streamers. The parents were <u>glad</u> to help clean up.

   Who is feeling happier? How do you know?

   _____

   _____

   _____

2. The patient <u>suspected</u> he might have a cold. The doctor <u>knew</u> it was just allergies.

   Who is more certain? How do you know?

   _____

   _____

   _____

3. I was <u>nervous</u> about dancing in front of my class. During the performance, I was <u>calm</u>.

   When is the dancer more afraid? How do you know?

   _____

   _____

   _____

On Your Own

In small groups, read each sentence. Circle the word that tells the correct answer. Use a dictionary if necessary.

Example:

Daniel was _____ when his new phone was stolen.

Which word tells that Daniel was extremely upset?

(furious)   mad

Try these examples yourself.

1 Elodia _____ that her answers were correct.

Which word tells that Elodia is not completely certain?

knew   believed

2 The kittens were _____ after spending the day playing.

Which word tells that the kittens are extremely tired?

drowsy   sleepy   exhausted

3 Charlie was so certain he would win that he was _____.

Which word tells that the boy is not at all polite?

bold   rude   cheeky

Complete the following activities.

4 If you are very upset about something new you learn, you might say you are

    A puzzled.

    B confused.

    C surprised.

    D shocked.

5 Read the sentence below.

    The student _____ the correct answer was in the book.

    Which words tell you the student was most certain of the answer?

    A believed that

    B suspected that

    C heard that

    D knew that

6 Describe the difference between the words *upset* and *angry*.

_____

_____

7 Read the sentences below.

    The <u>quiet</u> child sat in the corner.
    The <u>calm</u> child sat in the corner.

    Explain the difference in meaning between these two sentences.

_____

_____

8 Put the words below in the correct order, according to the shade of meaning. Some words have been defined for you.

melancholy				

happy

indifferent (not interested, does not care)

melancholy (very sad)

elated (very happy and excited)

sad

Critical Thinking

9 A thesaurus is a dictionary or an online list of words that have similar meanings. In a small group, investigate the shades of meaning in words you find in a thesaurus. You can use a thesaurus in book form or one you find online. Your word-processing program may have a built-in thesaurus. Compare them and discuss which is best to use. Then look up some common words that you use all the time in writing, such as come, *go*, *look*, *speak*, and *talk*. Pick one word that has a very good span of synonyms and make flash cards for them. Invite classmates to help you arrange those synonyms into groups that make sense, for example, "angry words," "soft words," "fast-moving words."

L.3.4	Determine or clarify the meaning of unknown and multiple-meaning word and phrases based on grade 3 reading and content, choosing flexibly from a range of strategies.
	d. Use glossaries or beginning dictionaries, both print and digital, to determine or clarify the precise meaning of key words and phrases.
L.3.6	Acquire and use accurately grade-appropriate conversational, general academic, and domain-specific words and phrases, including those that signal spatial and temporal relationships.
CCR.L.4	Determine or clarify the meaning of unknown and multiple-meaning words and phrases by using context clues, analyzing meaningful word parts, and consulting general and specialized reference materials, as appropriate.
CCR.L.6	Acquire and use accurately a range of general academic and domain-specific words and phrases sufficient for reading, writing, speaking, and listening at the college and career readiness level; demonstrate independence in gathering vocabulary knowledge when encountering an unknown term important to comprehension or expression.

Understand the Standards

Sometimes when you are reading, you will come across words you do not know:

> The baker was furious.

You can use a dictionary to find out what *furious* means.

- A **dictionary** tells what words mean. Dictionaries list words in alphabetical order.

To find a word in the dictionary:

1. Look at the first three letters in the word: *fur-*

2. Look at the guide words at the top of each page. **Guide words** tell you which words fall on the page. For example, *furious* falls between the words *fur* and *furrow*. The top of the page might look like this: fur • furrow. All the words on that page would fall between those two words in the alphabet.

3. Find the word, looking for words that begin with *fur-, then furi-*.

4. Read the dictionary entry:

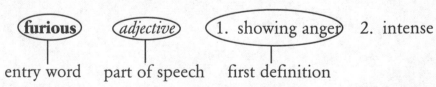

furious   adjective   1. showing anger   2. intense

   entry word   part of speech   first definition

A **thesaurus** has both definitions and synonyms, or words with similar meanings. If you wanted to find synonyms for *angry*, you could look in a thesaurus. A thesaurus also lists words in alphabetical order.

Words to Know

dictionary

guide words

thesaurus

Guided Instruction

Complete the activities that follow.

Draw a circle around the guide words you would find on the page for the entry word *dreadful*.

dinner • distant   (draw • dream)   drop • dry

Try these examples yourself.

1. Draw a circle around the guide words you would find on the page for the entry word *sink*.

silk • sip   stamp • still   ship • shore

2. Read these dictionary entries. Write two meanings for the multiple-meaning word *sink*. One should be a verb, and one should be a noun.

Dictionary entry:

sink *verb* 1 a. to go to the bottom b. to fall or drop to a lower place
sink *noun* a basin with a drain

_____

_____

_____

_____

_____

Writing Connection

3. Read this thesaurus entry:

> **quarrel** *verb* argue, bicker, fight, spat

a. Tell two words that are synonyms for *quarrel*.

_____

b. What part of speech is *quarrel* in this entry? _____

On Your Own

Discuss

In small groups, read each entry. Complete the activities that follow.

Example:

Thesaurus Entry:

>   **dreadful** *adjective* very bad: appalling, awful, fearful, frightful, horrible, shocking, terrible

Writing Connection

Write a sentence using two synonyms from the entry.

Daniel thought the play was horrible and the ending was terrible.

Try these examples yourself.

1 Dictionary Entry:

>   **present** *noun* 1. a gift 2. at this time, now

a. Which meaning of the word is used in this sentence? Explain.

   She brought her friend a birthday present.

_____

_____

b. Write two sentences, each using the word *present* in a different way.

   1. _____

   2. _____

2 Thesaurus Entry:

>   **happy** *adjective* being or showing good spirits: bright, cheerful, cheery, sunny

a. Write a sentence using two synonyms for *happy*.

_____

Complete the activities below.

3 Which guide words would be on the top of the page with the word *drape* on it?

A drama • draw   **C** dome • door

B dream • drive   **D** dart • dance

4 Read the dictionary entry below.

grant *verb* 1. to allow something

What is the circled part of the entry?

A a guide word   **C** the part of speech

B the entry word   **D** the definition

5 Read the dictionary entry below.

free *adjective* 1. no cost. 2. not in use
free *verb* 1. get rid of. 2. release

Which meaning of *free* is correct in this sentence? Explain how you know.

We did not have any money, so we could only go on the <u>free</u> rides.

_____

_____

6 What is one time when you might use a dictionary? Explain how it would be helpful.

_____

_____

 7 You are writing a story and you want to find just the right word to describe your main character. How could you use a thesaurus to help you? How could you use a dictionary?

_____

_____

Make Multiple-Meaning Flashcards

Use 5 x 7 inch note cards to make a game for your classmates. In a small group, think of five multiple-meaning words. Use a print or online dictionary to help you. Write each word on two note cards. On the back, write a definition. Each card should have a different definition. You should have ten cards total.

Swap your cards with another group's. Turn the cards definition side up. Then, match the cards until you have five pairs. Check your work by turning the cards over. Each pair should have the same multiple-meaning word on it.

not very heavy	not dark

Perform a Skit on Idioms

If someone tells you she has a bad taste in her mouth, she *might* mean she just ate something bad, but more likely, she means she is upset at someone's actions. English is full of phrases whose meanings cannot be guessed by knowing the meaning of the words. You just have to memorize these.

In a small group, look online for a list of idioms and their meanings. Write a skit (a short play) that includes six idioms. Use action to help the class understand what the idiom means. Discuss the idioms with the class after the performance. See how many they understood.

Create a Poster

Read the list of words below. Choose a word and think of an example from your own life that helps you understand the word.

lonely   bored   confused   angry   friendly   lazy

Once you've thought of your word and your example, make a poster to illustrate your word. Write the word at the top of the poster board. Then download and print images, draw, or paint things that help you understand the word. Share your poster with the class, and tell them about your example.

Write a Pamphlet

In a small group, brainstorm the top reasons to use reference materials. Write the top five reasons to use a dictionary or a thesaurus. (For example, you have forgotten how to say a word.) Discuss when you have used a dictionary or a thesaurus.

Then, fold a sheet of paper in half to make a pamphlet telling your reasons. On the left side, write your reasons. On the right side, illustrate your pamphlet with pictures from the Internet. Put your pamphlet on a class bulletin board.

Lesson 11

Parts of a Work

RL.3.5	Refer to parts of stories, dramas, and poems using terms such as chapter, scene, and stanza; describe how each successive part builds on earlier sections.
CCR.R.10	Read and comprehend complex literary and informational texts independently and proficiently.
CCR.SL.1	Prepare for and participate effectively in a range of conversations and collaborations with diverse partners, building on others' ideas and expressing their own clearly and persuasively.

Understand the Standards

Literature
Connection

You probably read all kinds of writing. You may have read stories or full-length books. You may have read short and long poems. You may have read or seen plays—or even acted in one yourself!

Words to Know
chapters
stanzas
scenes

A long work such as a book, long poem, or play is often divided into parts.

○ In a long story, the parts are called **chapters**. Each chapter tells something that happens in the story.

> Chapter 2
>
> Ana ran along the edge of the river. The baby deer in the water swam as hard as it could. It was getting tired, Ana could tell. She had to help the poor fawn!

○ In a long poem, the parts are called **stanzas**. Each stanza is a group of lines. Usually stanzas in a poem have the same number of lines.

> The night was dark, the wind was soft
> The stars danced in the sky
> And far below an orange moon
> I heard an owl's cry.

○ In a play, the parts are called **scenes**. Each scene helps move the action of the play along.

> Scene 3. *[Maria's kitchen.]*
> MARIA: Oh no! The pie is burned!

Dividing a long work into parts makes it easier to read. Each part leads into the next part. This makes the reader want to read on.

Guided Instruction

Discuss

A book, poem, or play tells a story. Each part of the work tells a part of a story. The next part of the work builds on the excitement of the last part.

To tell what the part of a work you are reading is called, you have to think about what kind of work it is.

Example: Lori and Tomas walked for a long time. They were very hot and tired. The path got harder and harder to follow. All at once Lori stopped. "I think we are lost," she said in a shaky voice.

Think: This is part of a story. It must be a chapter.

Try these examples yourself.

1. SARAH: Have you seen my dog? He ran away. I am trying to find him.
   MR. BRIDGE: He's here, all right. I've spent all day teaching him some manners!

   Think: _____

2. Adam stood on the diving board, looking down. The water was very far away. He could hear his friends calling, "Dive! Dive!" He closed his eyes, raised his arms, and jumped.

   Think: _____

3. The wild horses turned and then
   They ran across the plain.
   In just a moment they were gone
   And never seen again.

   Think: _____

On Your Own

Read the passage on your own. Decide the kind of text it is. Then work with a partner to answer the questions that follow.

[Ms. Ruiz's classroom. Students are standing around the teacher's desk.]

TONY: Look, there is something strange on Ms. Ruiz's desk. What do you think it could be?

SELMA: It looks like a box, but I think there might be something inside it.

JENNA: Why is there a towel over it, and why is it moving?

MS. RUIZ: All right, students, it is time to sit down and be quiet, please.

JENNA: Ms. Ruiz, is there something alive in the box on your desk?

MS. RUIZ: I will show you as soon as you are all quiet. *[The students sit down, and she takes the towel off the box.]*

TONY: Hey, is that really a rabbit? What is it doing in our classroom?

SELMA: Does it have a name, or do we get to name it ourselves? Can we keep it, please?

MS. RUIZ: This is our new class pet, and she already has a name–Pearl. She will live in our classroom on school days, and we can take turns taking her home on the weekends.

Answer the questions based on the passage.

1 What is this kind of work called?

_____

2 What is this part of the work called?

_____

3 Where does the scene take place?

    A in a bedroom

    B in a classroom

    C on a playground

    D in a lunchroom

4 What part of the work would come next?

    A Scene 4

    B Chapter 2

    C Stanza 3

    D Chapter 5

5 How do the students feel about the rabbit?

_____

6 You can read this scene. What else can you do with it?

_____

 7 Work in a small group. Discuss and decide what might happen in the next scene. Then, on your own paper, write your version of the scene. Next, compare your version with the versions of the other group members. Work together to create a final version you all agree on. Present it to the class.

RL.3.1	Ask and answer questions to demonstrate understanding of a text referring explicitly to the text as the basis for the answers.
SL.3.1	Engage effectively in a range of collaborative discussions with diverse partners on grade 3 topics and texts, building on others' ideas and expressing their own clearly.
	c. Ask questions to check understanding of information presented, stay on topic, and link their comments to the remarks of others.
CCR.R.1	Read closely to determine what the text says explicitly and to make logical inferences from it; cite specific textual evidence when writing or speaking to support conclusions drawn from the text.
CCR.SL.1	Prepare for and participate effectively in a range of conversations and collaborations with diverse partners, building on others' ideas and expressing their own clearly and persuasively.
CCR.W.9	Draw evidence from literary or informational texts to support analysis, reflection, and research.
L.3.3	Use knowledge of language and its conventions when writing, speaking, reading, or listening.

Understand the Standards

Imagine you are reading a story called "The Noise in the Night." You read this paragraph:

> **Words to Know**
> draw conclusions

> Margo tiptoed down the stairs, shining the flashlight in front of her. The terrible voice came again: "Who?" it moaned. "Whoooo?"

You might ask yourself questions such as: What is moaning? What will happen to Margo?

When you read stories at school, your teacher may ask you questions about them. You may ask yourself questions as you read too. Asking and answering questions about a story can help you understand it more fully.

You can ask and answer questions at different times when you read.

- Ask and answer before reading to help you get ready to read.
  What does the title tell me about the story?

- Ask and answer during reading to help you understand as you read.
  What does the main character want?

- Ask and answer after reading to help you understand what you have read.
  Why did the story end that way?

You can find the answers to your questions in different ways. You can look in the text for the answer. You can think about what you already know to find the answer. You can **draw conclusions**, or use clues in the text to make a good guess about the answer.

Guided Instruction

When you read a story, think about the title and what happens. Ask and answer questions to understand the story.

The Magic Coin

Andi skipped down the sidewalk. Something shiny on the ground caught her eye, and she stopped to look more closely at it.

"Why, it's a coin!" Andi exclaimed, picking it up. It didn't look like any coin she had ever seen. There was a strange animal stamped on it, a kind of horse with a horn on its forehead.

Andi turned the coin over and over, wondering what it was. Then she slipped it in her pocket. It was getting very hot out, and she thought, "I wish I were in the swimming pool!"

Guided Questions

What does the title tell about the story?

_____

_____

What is the animal on the coin?

_____

Write two more questions about the story and answer them.

1. Question: _____

   _____

   Answer: _____

   _____

2. Question: _____

   _____

   Answer: _____

   _____

On Your Own

Collaborative Learning

Read the part of a story. Work with a partner to ask and answer the kinds of questions described below.

A Wet Surprise

Jonah and his mother ran as fast as they could through the pouring rain. They threw open the car doors and jumped inside, shivering and dripping.

"Oh no, I left my window down, and my seat is all wet!" Jonah's mother exclaimed.

Suddenly Jonah heard a bark. Right next to him, on the floor of the car, was a little dog. It had bright eyes and wiry hair and a funny face. Jonah's mother looked in the back, her mouth open in shock.

"Where on Earth did that dog come from?" she asked.

Jonah reached out a hand, and the dog licked it, its stumpy little tail wagging hard. "It likes me, Mom!" he cried. "Look, it doesn't have a collar, so it must be lost. Please, can we keep it?"

Complete these activities based on the passage you just read.

1 Write a question that you can use the text to answer.

_____

_____

2 Write a question that you have to use your own knowledge to answer.

_____

3 What is the surprise in the title?

A a car

B a rainstorm

C a dog

D an argument

4 How does Jonah feel about the dog?

    A He is afraid of it.

    B He doesn't like it.

    C He feels sorry for it.

    D He likes it.

5 Does the dog belong to Jonah? How do you know?

_____

_____

6 Write a question that might help you understand how Jonah feels.

_____

Elevate 7 On your own sheet of paper, ask and answer a question about the dog and the car. Draw a conclusion in your answer. Use clues from the text to support your conclusion. Then discuss your question and conclusion with a partner. Defend your response with information from the text.

_____

_____

_____

RL.3.2	Recount stories, including fables, folktales, and myths from diverse cultures; determine the central message, lesson, or moral and explain how it is conveyed through key details in the text.
RL.3.10	By the end of the year, read and comprehend literature, including stories, dramas, and poetry, at the high end of the grades 2–3 text complexity band independently and proficiently.
SL.3.4	Report on a topic or text, tell a story, or recount an experience with appropriate facts and details, speaking clearly at an understandable pace.
CCR.R.2	Determine central ideas or themes of a text and analyze their development; summarize the key supporting details and ideas.
CCR.SL.1	Prepare for and participate effectively in a range of conversations and collaborations with diverse partners, building on others' ideas and expressing their own clearly and persuasively.
CCR.SL.4	Present information, findings, and supporting evidence such that listeners can follow the line of reasoning and the organization, development, and style are appropriate to task, purpose, and audience.

Understand the Standards

Literature Connection

Imagine that you have read a story that was really interesting, and your teacher asks you what it was about. You don't want to tell every single detail of the story—that would take forever!

Words to Know
retell
summary

You can **retell** the story in your own words. In a retelling, you give a **summary**, or a short statement of the most important things that happen. Your retelling should include:

- the name of the original story

- the most important characters (people or animals), ideas, and events in the story

- details about the characters, ideas, and events

- the message or lesson, if the story has one

In the story "Beauty and the Beast," Beauty has to live with the terrible Beast to save her father's life. Over time, though, she learns that the Beast is actually kind and generous. She falls in love with the Beast. Her love breaks the spell the Beast was under, and she discovers that he is a prince. She learns that you cannot tell what a person is like by his looks.

Guided Instruction

When you retell a story, you should include only the most important details. Leave out details that do not tell about the characters, central ideas, events, and message.

Literature Connection

Read the retelling. Think about the characters, the events, and the message.

"The Tortoise and the Hare" by Aesop is about a hare who is very boastful. He tells a tortoise he has never lost a race. A tortoise is similar to a turtle. The hare challenges the tortoise to a race with him, and the tortoise agrees.

The race starts, and the hare takes off fast. Before long he is so far ahead that he stops to take a nap. The other animals watch the race. As the hare sleeps, the tortoise creeps slowly on. Before long, the tortoise passes the hare and keeps on going. The tortoise wins the race. He is not even tired at the end. When the hare wakes up, he is shocked to find out that he has lost the race. He learns that it is more important to keep going than to be fast.

Guided Questions

How much of the race is summarized in paragraph 2?

_____

_____

Does the story have a message? What is it?

_____

_____

_____

Answer the questions based on the passage.

1. What is the title of the story being retold?

_____

2. What is the first detail that does not belong in the retelling?

_____

3. Which of these details does not belong in the retelling?

   A He challenges the tortoise to a race with him, and the tortoise agrees.

   B The race starts, and the hare takes off fast.

   C The other animals watch the race.

   D As the hare sleeps, the tortoise passes him, and the tortoise wins the race.

4. Why is it important that the hare stops to take a nap?

_____

5. What other detail does not belong in the retelling?

 On Your Own

Look at these story retellings. Find the detail in each retelling that is not important. Cross it out.

1 In "The Magic Fish," a fisherman catches a strange fish. It grants the fisherman three wishes. The fish is at least two feet long.

2 The story "Half Magic" is about four children who find a magic coin. The coin is not a nickel or a dime. It gives them half of each wish they make.

3 "The Little Mermaid" is a tale about a mermaid who falls in love with a human prince. The mermaid and prince marry. There is a movie about the little mermaid.

Complete the following activity.

 4 Work with a partner. Reread and discuss a story you both have read and liked. Then work together to write a short retelling of it. Be sure to include the four things listed on the first page of this lesson. Make sure you agree on every statement you include.

Lesson 14

Understanding Character

RL.3.3   Describe characters in a story and explain how their actions contribute to the sequence of events.
CCR.R.3   Analyze how and why individuals, events, and ideas develop and interact over the course of a text.
CCR.SL.1   Prepare for and participate effectively in a range of conversations and collaborations with diverse partners, building on others' ideas and expressing their own clearly and persuasively.
CCR.W.9   Draw evidence from literary or informational texts to support analysis, reflection, and research.

 Understand the Standards

The people or animals that a story or play is about are called characters. The most important character in a work is called the **main character**.

> **Words to Know**
> main character
> traits
> motivations

When you read about characters, you should think about what they do and why they act the way they do. You can learn about characters from what the writer tells you directly about them. You can also learn about them from what they do, what they say, and what other characters say about them. Pay attention to:

- the character's **traits,** or special qualities of his or her personality

    Some possible traits: *confidence, shyness, friendliness, bravery*

- the character's feelings or emotions

    Some possible feelings: *sadness, anger, joy, curiosity, fear*

- the character's **motivations,** or reasons for acting

    Some possible motivations: *wanting to help, fear of strangers, love of nature*

Guided Instruction

When you read about a character, ask yourself what the character is like. Think about his or her traits, feelings, and motivations. Look for information from the writer or other characters and the actions and words of the character.

Jamal lay on the couch, exhausted. He had been working in his mother's garden all day, so when his friend Andy came over and invited him to go for a hike, Jamal did not really want to go.

"It's hot out, and I am very tired," Jamal said.

"Oh, please come! We can hike to the lake and go swimming," Andy begged.

Jamal hated to disappoint Andy, and the lake sounded great. He got to his feet. "Okay, let's go!" he agreed.

Guided Questions

What do you think Jamal looks like as he lies on the couch?

_____

_____

_____

Why do you think Jamal hated to disappoint Andy?

_____

_____

_____

What do you think most made Jamal agree to go with Andy?

_____

_____

_____

Fill in the web with character traits, motivations, and feelings. The first one has been done for you.

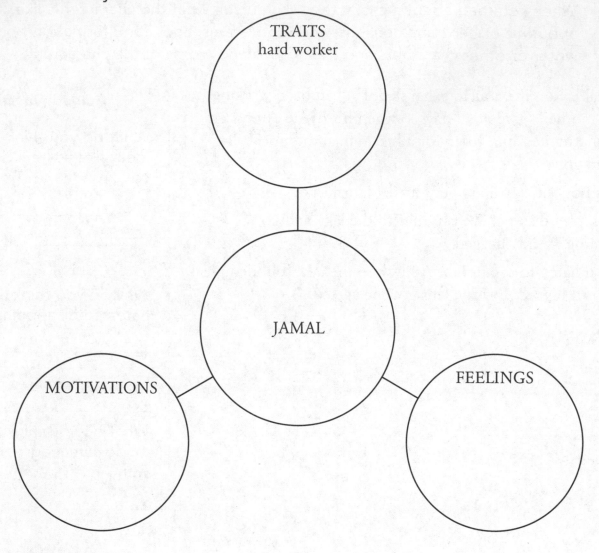

TRAITS
hard worker

JAMAL

MOTIVATIONS

FEELINGS

On Your Own

Read the passage. Work with your partner to answer the questions about Tia's character traits, motivations, and feelings.

Social Studies Connection

Tia for President!

"I think you should run for class president, Tia!" said Will as they ate their sandwiches in the lunchroom.

"You know how much I hate talking in front of people," Tia protested. "I'd be terrible!"

"You'd be amazing," Will stated confidently. "You're smart and you care about people, and you have lots of great ideas. Don't you want to help our class?"

Measuring Up® to the Common Core

Tia thought about Will's question. She would have to give a speech in front of everyone. Everyone would be looking at her. But she did want to help the class, and her idea about having a class talent show to raise money for a trip to the Natural History Museum was pretty good.

"I guess I could try," Tia said at last. "Would you help me?"

"Of course I would," Will said. "We'll make a great team!"

Answer the questions based on the passage. Complete the activities.

1 Who is the main character in the story? _____

2 What is Tia's motivation for deciding to run for class president?

_____

3 Will says that Tia is

A brave.

B smart.

C a good speaker.

D talented.

4 How does Tia feel about giving a speech?

A fearful

B confident

C happy

D curious

5 You can tell that Tia is a caring person because she

_____

6 What do Tia's feelings about giving a speech show about her?

_____

Discuss

7 On a separate sheet of paper, tell if you agree that Tia will make a good class president. Why or why not? Then compare your response with a classmate's. Find where you agree and disagree. Then try to reach a common conclusion.

Critical Thinking

8 In a small group, list and rank the five most interesting main characters in TV shows that you all watch and books you enjoy. Pick four of each. Then list the character traits that they have in common and character traits that are different. Then pick two characters who could never have met in real life. Work together to create an interesting possible conversation between them. Enact completed conversations in front of your classmates.

 Measuring Up® to the Common Core

RL.3.3	Describe characters in a story and explain how their actions contribute to the sequence of events.
CCR.R.3	Analyze how and why individuals, events, and ideas develop and interact over the course of a text.
CCR.W.9	Draw evidence from literary or informational texts to support analysis, reflection, and research.

 ## Understand the Standards

When you talk about a story in class, you may describe its **plot**. The plot is the plan of a story. It gives a story a beginning, a middle, and an end. It usually describes a **problem**, or difficulty, the main character faces and the **solution**, or answer, to the problem.

> **Words to Know**
> plot
> problem
> solution
> sequence of events
> climax

The **sequence of events** in a plot is the order in which things happen. Notice what happens first, second, next, and last.

When you think about plot, pay attention to:

- the beginning, which introduces the characters and the problem.

- the middle, which tells how the characters try to solve the problem. It includes the **climax**, or the most exciting moment.

- the end, which tells how the characters solve the problem.

Guided Instruction

When you read a story, notice the events that happen and the order in which they happen. Think about the problem the characters face and how they solve it.

Bird on the Loose

"Simon, you have to help me—Charlie has gotten out of his cage!" Abby said frantically. The parrot flew wildly around the room as Abby chased him.

Simon waved his arms, trying to make Charlie fly toward Abby. The bird just grew more frightened. Suddenly his wing brushed against a vase. The vase fell over and broke with a crash, and Abby screamed.

"Get a mirror!" Simon cried. Abby brought in a little mirror and held it up. Charlie saw his reflection in the mirror as he flew past. He was curious about the other bird he saw—his own reflection. He landed on a table, and, still holding the mirror, Abby gently picked him up and put him back in his cage.

Guided Questions

Who are the three characters in the story? How do you know one is a bird?

_____

_____

_____

What words does the writer use to create a feeling of excitement as the story unfolds?

_____

_____

_____

How do you know when the characters have reached a solution?

_____

_____

_____

Answer and discuss these questions about the passage.

1. What happens first?

_____

2. What is the climax of the story?

_____

3. What happens after Charlie sees himself in the mirror?

_____

On Your Own

Collaborative Learning

Read the passage. Think about the plot events. Then work with a partner to fill in the chart with events from the story in the order in which they happen.

Danger on the Lake

The little sailboat skimmed over the water in the strong breeze. "See, I told you I was a good sailor!" Antwon boasted.

"We're really going fast!" Michael said. "It's great, but is that a rain cloud?" The sky had suddenly gotten darker, and now the wind was blowing hard.

"I'll turn the boat around, and we'll go back," Antwon said. But the wind was too strong, and he couldn't control the boat. Suddenly it tilted, and the boys shouted in fear.

"Head for the shore!" Michael cried. "We're going to turn over if we stay here!" Antwon steered the boat to the nearest shore, and it scraped onto the sand just as the skies opened and the rain poured down.

"I guess I could use a few more lessons," Antwon said sheepishly, as the raindrops dripped off his nose.

beginning _____

_____

middle _____

_____

end _____

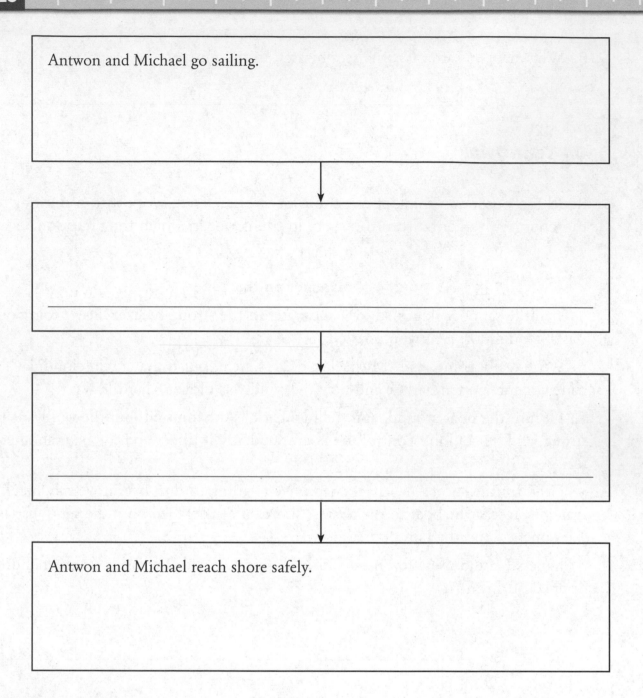

Antwon and Michael go sailing.

Antwon and Michael reach shore safely.

Answer the questions based on the passage.

1 What is the climax of the story?

   A The boys enjoy their sail.

   B Michael sees a rain cloud.

   C Antwon boasts about sailing.

   D The boat tilts suddenly.

2 What problem do the characters face?

    A Their boat is sinking.

    B A storm is coming.

    C They do not know how to sail.

    D They are lost.

3 What happens after the wind gets stronger?

_____

_____

4 How does Antwon make the problem more serious?

_____

 5 On a separate sheet of paper, write another solution to the problem that Antwon and Michael face.

Lesson 16

Understanding Point of View

RL.3.6	Distinguish their own point of view from that of the narrator or those of the characters.
CCR.R.6	Assess how point of view or purpose shapes the content and style of a text.
CCR.SL.3	Evaluate a speaker's point of view, reasoning, and use of evidence and rhetoric.

 Understand the Standards

When you read a story for class, you might talk about who tells the story. The person who tells a story is the **narrator**. Sometimes the narrator is a person in the story. Other times, the narrator may be a person outside the story who is telling the story.

> **Words to Know**
> narrator
> third-person point of view
> first-person point of view

- Some stories use **third-person point of view**. In these stories, the narrator is not a character in the story.

  Naomi pointed her snowboard down the hill. Then she started to slide. Before long, she was zipping down the slope.

Third-person point of view uses the words *he* and *she* to refer to characters. It often gives you information about all the characters in a story.

- Some stories use **first-person point of view**. In these stories, the narrator is a character in the story.

  I pointed my snowboard down the hill. Then I started to slide. Before long, I was zipping down the slope.

First-person point of view uses the words *I* and *me*. It tells the story through the narrator's eyes.

74 English Language Arts — Level C   Copying is illegal.   Measuring Up® to the Common Core

Guided Instruction

When you read a story, think about who is telling the story. Look for how the words *he* and *she* or *I* and *me* are used.

from "Jack and the Beanstalk"

Jack was on his way to market to sell his cow, Bessie. The cow was old and she took her time walking along the road. Jack pulled and yanked at the rope, but Bessie did not want to speed up. She chewed on flowers at the edge of the road, ignoring her owner.

They passed a woman sitting by the side of the road. "Young man," she called. "I will trade you that beautiful cow for these beans!" Jack was so annoyed at Bessie that he hurried over to the woman. She held out a handful of beans.

Guided Questions
When you read the first paragraph, is someone inside the story or outside the story telling you what happened? How do you know?
_____
_____
_____
_____
What do the narrator's eyes see in this paragraph?
_____
_____
_____
When the woman in the last paragraph uses *I*, does she become a first-person narrator?
_____
_____
_____

Answer the questions about the story.

1. What does the narrator tell you about Bessie?

_____

2. What point of view does the story use?

_____

3. What words tell you about the point of view?

_____

 On Your Own

 Read the passage. Think about the narrator and what the narrator tells you. Then work with a partner to complete the activities that follow.

Discuss

Rapunzel's Tower

Literature Connection

    I had lived alone in a tower for as long as I could remember. My only friends were the birds that sometimes perched on the high windowsill. How lonely I was, and how I longed to see another human being!

    One spring afternoon I got my wish. There, in the field below, was a boy. He was dressed like a prince, in rich velvet. "Hello," I called out.

    The boy looked around, and then he looked up. His mouth dropped open at the sight of me leaning out the tower window, my long golden braid hanging nearly to the ground.

    "Who are you, and what are you doing up there?" he cried, running to the foot of the tower.

    "I am Rapunzel and I live here!" I said, so thrilled I could barely speak.

Complete these activities based on the passage you just read.

1 Who is the narrator in the story?

_____

2 What point of view does the story use? How do you know?

_____

3 What character in the story do you learn most about? Why?

_____

4 The narrator describes herself as

   A lonely.

   B princely.

   C surprised.

   D confused.

5 Which of the following best describes the story's narrator?

   A a prince

   B outside the story

   C at the center of the action

   D an unimportant character

6 Why don't you know very much about the boy in the story?

_____

_____

7 If the story were written from the boy's point of view, what might you know?

_____

 8 How would this story be different if it were written in the third-person point of view? On a separate sheet of paper, explain the differences. Then work with a partner to write a third-person version of the story. Agree on the changes you need to make.

Lesson 17

Understanding Theme

RL.3.2	Recount stories, including fables, folktales, and myths from diverse cultures; determine the central message, lesson, or moral, and explain how it is conveyed through key details in the text.
RL.3.10	By the end of the year, read and comprehend literature, including stories, dramas, and poetry, at the high end of the grades 2–3 text complexity band independently and proficiently.
CCR.R.2	Determine central ideas or themes of a text and analyze their development; summarize the key supporting details and ideas.
CCR.W.9	Draw evidence from literary or informational texts to support analysis, reflection, and research.

Understand the Standards

Real World Connection

In school and in the work world, you are always learning lessons about life. Stories can have lessons about life too. When you read a story, think about its big idea, or **theme**. The theme teaches you something about life.

> **Words to Know**
> theme

Some stories, such as fables, come right out and tell you the theme.

> Look before you leap.

> Don't count your chickens before they are hatched.

> Honesty is the best policy.

In other stories, the theme is not always obvious. For example, you might read a story about a girl who is kind to a new student. Later, when the girl needs help, the student helps her. The theme of this story might be:

> Kindness is often returned.

To figure out the theme of a story, do the following:

○ Identify the main character and the problem.

○ Notice how the main character solves the problem.

○ Think about what the character learns from the problem.

○ Connect what the character learns—the big idea—to your own life.

Guided Instruction

When you read a story, think about the main character and the problem. Decide what the character learns and how he or she changes. Then find the theme.

Multicultural Connection

"The Lion and the Mouse" by Aesop

Once there was a little Mouse who was in a great hurry. By accident, he ran over a Lion's paw, waking the great beast. The Lion opened his mouth to eat the Mouse.

"Oh, please spare me," cried the Mouse. "If you do, I will find a way to do you a favor in the future!" The Lion was amused by the idea that the Mouse could help him, so he let the little creature go.

A few weeks later, the Lion was captured and tied up by hunters. As he struggled, the Mouse came to him and chewed through the ropes. "You were right," the Lion said. "Your favor to me was at least as great as mine to you!"

Who are the main characters? How are they different?

_____

_____

What words tell you that the theme or moral is being told to you directly?

_____

_____

How could the theme apply to your life?

_____

_____

_____

Answer the questions about the story.

1. What problem does the Lion face?

_____

2. What is the solution to the problem?

_____

3. What does the Lion learn in the story?

_____

_____

On Your Own

Read this story from India. Think about the problem the main character faces and how he solves it. Consider the story's big idea, or theme.

Multicultural
Connection

The Lightning Bug and the Jackdaw

A jackdaw flew up to a lightning bug and was about to swallow him. The lightning bug was terrified. He knew he had to do something, though the jackdaw was much bigger and stronger than he was.

"Wait a minute," said the lightning bug. "I know where you can find many, many lightning bugs like me. Wouldn't you rather have a feast?"

"Yes, indeed I would!" cried the jackdaw hungrily. The lightning bug flew into the forest, and the jackdaw flapped heavily behind him, thinking about the delicious meal to come. They came to a place where travelers had lighted a fire. Sparks flew up from the fire, looking exactly like tiny lightning bugs flitting about.

"There they are," said the lightning bug. "Enjoy your meal!"

The jackdaw darted forward and tried to swallow a spark, but it burned her mouth so badly she cried out. "Oh," she said, "you lightning bugs are not as tasty as you look!"

Answer the questions based on the passage.

1 What problem does the lightning bug face?

_____

2 What is the solution to the problem?

_____

3 What does the lightning bug learn?

_____

4 How would you describe the jackdaw?

   A strong and brave

   B smart and cunning

   C honest and trustworthy

   D greedy and foolish

5 Why is the lightning bug able to solve the problem?

_____

6 What is the theme of the story?

_____

Writing Connection

7 On a separate sheet of paper, write how you might connect the theme of "The Lightning Bug and the Jackdaw" to your own life.

RL.3.9	Compare and contrast the themes, settings, and plots of stories written by the same author about the same or similar characters.
RL.3.10	By the end of the year, read and comprehend literature, including stories, dramas, and poetry, at the high end of the grades 2–3 text complexity band independently and proficiently.
CCR.R.9	Analyze how two or more texts address similar themes or topics in order to build knowledge or to compare the approaches the authors take.
CCR.W.9	Draw evidence from literary or informational texts to support analysis, reflection, and research.

Understand the Standards

One way to learn more about a story you have read for a class is to compare and contrast it with other stories. When you **compare** stories, you show how they are alike. When you **contrast** stories, you show how they are different.

Words to Know

compare
contrast

Literature
Connection

Sometimes you will read stories by the same writer. You can do the following:

○ Compare and contrast plots, showing how the events are alike and different.

Both *The Lion, the Witch, and the Wardrobe* and *Prince Caspian* by C. S. Lewis are about a fight against an evil enemy. In the first book, the enemy is a terrible witch. In the second book, the enemy is a cruel king.

○ Compare and contrast themes, explaining how the writer expresses the theme in each story.

Both *Dear Mr. Henshaw* and *Ellen Tebbits* by Beverly Cleary teach the theme of accepting yourself. Leigh, in *Dear Mr. Henshaw*, learns to accept himself by writing to a famous author, while Ellen Tebbits learns self-acceptance by dealing with a bully.

○ Compare and contrast characters, showing how a writer might write about the same character or similar characters, or how the characters are different.

The Saturdays and *The Four-Story Mistake* by Elizabeth Enright are about the same four children: Mona, Rush, Miranda, and Oliver. In the second book, the children are older and wiser.

 Measuring Up® to the Common Core

Guided Instruction

When you compare and contrast stories, you must think about their plots, themes, and characters. Consider how they are the same and different.

Mina's Overnight

Mina had never spent the night away from home before. She was very excited as she packed her bag. She waved good-bye to her parents and climbed into her friend Allison's car.

Before the car had gone two blocks, though, Mina was homesick. By the time they got to Allison's house, she found she couldn't get out of the car.

"Will you take me home?" she asked Allison and her parents. "I love visiting your house, but I don't think I'm ready to sleep away from my own home and my parents."

The Dance Recital

Allison was terribly nervous about the dance recital. "I'm not ready!" she told her mother, but her mother didn't believe her.

When it was time for Allison to go onstage, she felt frozen and couldn't move. Another dancer performed instead. Afterward, Allison's mother hugged her. "You were right," she said. "You just weren't ready!"

Guided Questions

Why was Mina excited in the beginning?

_____

_____

_____

How are Mina and Allison different?

_____

_____

_____

_____

_____

The writer describes Allison as feeling "frozen." Is Mina also "frozen"? Why or why not?

_____

_____

_____

_____

Answer the questions about the stories.

1. How are the characters in the stories alike and different?

_____

_____

2. What theme do both stories share?

_____

_____

On Your Own

Multicultural Connection

Read the two fables by Aesop. Think about how the plots and characters are alike and different. Then work with a partner to fill in the Venn diagram. Write the ways the plots and characters are different in the parts of the ovals that do not overlap. Write the ways they are alike in the parts that do overlap.

The Vain Jackdaw

The jackdaw wanted to be king of the birds, but he knew that Jupiter would not choose him unless he was beautiful. He walked all through the woods and meadows, picking up feathers from other birds and sticking them on himself.

The day came for Jupiter to choose, and he chose the jackdaw. But the other birds turned to the jackdaw and plucked their feathers from him. The jackdaw was left in his own feathers, only a plain jackdaw after all.

The Peacock and the Crane

A peacock spread its beautiful tail as a crane passed nearby. "I am so much lovelier than you," he said. "My tail is all the colors of the rainbow, while you are feathered only in white."

"That is true," the crane replied. "Yet I can fly above the clouds, and you—you can only walk on the earth. You are hardly a bird at all."

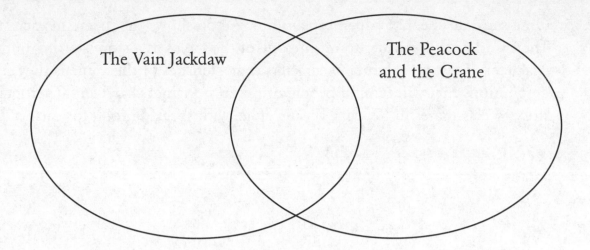

Complete the following activities based on the fables you just read.

1 Who is the main character of "The Vain Jackdaw"?

    A a crane

    B a peacock

    C a jackdaw

    D Jupiter

2 How are the jackdaw and the peacock alike?

    A They think they are better than they really are.

    B They are both very beautiful.

    C They want to be king of the birds.

    D Neither of them can fly.

3 How are the plots of the two stories alike?

    _____

    _____

4 What theme do both stories share?

    _____

    _____

Critical Thinking

5 On a separate sheet of paper, explain how Aesop shows the theme in each story. Then work with a partner to rewrite one of the fables as a story starring human characters. Give your human characters characteristics of the animals they replace. Use descriptions that will remind people of Aesop's original characters. Then present your story to classmates in Readers Theater style, with speaking roles for each of you.

RL.3.7	Use information gained from illustrations and the words in a text to demonstrate understanding of the text.
RL.3.10	By the end of the year, read and comprehend literature, including stories, dramas, and poetry, at the high end of the grades 2–3 text complexity band independently and proficiently.
CCR.R.7	Integrate and evaluate content presented in diverse media and formats, including visually and quantitatively, as well as in words.
L.3.3	Use knowledge of language and its conventions when writing, speaking, reading, or listening. **a.** Choose words and phrases for effect.

Understand the Standards

Music/Arts Connection

Some stories that you read for class may have **illustrations**. Looking carefully at the illustrations can help you understand the story more fully.

Words to Know

illustrations

- Illustrations of characters can show you what the characters look like, how they feel, or what they are doing.

- Illustrations of the setting can tell you about the time and place of the story.

- Illustrations of the events can help you figure out what happens in the story. They can also give a sense of the mood of the story.

This illustration, for example, shows you that the story is set long ago, at night, during a rainstorm. It shows a knight and his horse. The knight looks worried as he knocks on a door. The mood in the illustration is one of danger.

Guided Instruction

When you look at a story's illustrations, think about what they show about the characters, setting, events, and mood.

Music/Arts Connection

In the Well

Sammy was yelling as he ran, so we had to listen carefully to figure out what was wrong. "Tiger is down the well!" he shouted. "We have to do something!"

We all ran to the old well, where we could hear Sammy's cat meowing desperately. Carmen had an idea. "Let's lower a box with some food in it," she said, "and Tiger will climb into the box to get the food."

We found a box, tied it to a rope, put some cat food in, and lowered it. Then we waited and worried. At last, Tiger stepped into the box and started to eat. Carefully, we raised the box and cheered. Tiger was saved!

Guided Questions

What does it look like the four people are doing?

_____

_____

Where does the story take place?

_____

_____

What makes you think that what they are pulling up is heavy?

_____

_____

_____

What part of the story does this illustration tell you more about?

_____

_____

_____

Answer the questions about the story.

1. What word in the story describes how the characters look in the illustration?

_____

2. What does the illustration show about the well?

_____

3. What mood does the illustration show?

_____

 On Your Own

Read the story and look at the illustration. Think about the characters, setting, events, and mood. Then fill in the chart with details from the story and the illustration that tell about the character and the setting.

Sudden Storm

Sasha didn't want to go back to the cabin. She had just finished a picnic lunch, and she just wanted to lie on the blanket and stare at the clouds. "All right," her mother said, "but it's supposed to rain!"

"I don't believe it—I'm staying here," Sasha told her.

It was calm and peaceful on the blanket for a while, but then Sasha noticed that the white, fluffy clouds overhead had darkened. Before she could pick up the blanket and start back, thunder boomed, and the sky opened. In an instant Sasha was soaked through, cold and miserable. She started to run, but she couldn't remember which path to take to get back to the cabin. She wasn't just wet— she was lost!

Scared and unhappy, Sasha stumbled through the woods. Before long, she heard someone calling her name. It was her mother, with an umbrella and a towel. Sasha ran to her and wrapped the towel around herself. "I'll believe you next time!" Sasha promised, shivering and laughing with relief.

	Character	Setting	Mood
Story details			
Illustration details			

 Measuring Up® to the Common Core

Answer the questions about a story that includes the illustration below.

1 Where is the story set?

   A in a living room

   B in a park

   C in a school

   D on a beach

2 How are the characters feeling?

   A They are sad and lonely.

   B They are angry at each other.

   C They are busy and involved.

   D They are afraid of something.

3 What do you think is happening in the story?

   _____

4 What mood does the illustration show?

   _____

5 On a separate sheet of paper, write a story telling what happens in the illustration.

Lesson 20

RL.3.4	Determine the meaning of words and phrases as they are used in a text, distinguishing literal from nonliteral language.
CCR.R.4	Interpret words and phrases as they are used in a text, including determining technical, connotative, and figurative meanings, and analyze how specific word choices shape meaning or tone.
L.3.3	Use knowledge of language and its conventions when writing, speaking, reading, or listening. **a.** Choose words and phrases for effect.

 Understand the Standards

Language Connection

When you read something for school or work, you may come across a word or phrase that seems strange. Imagine that you read the following sentence in a story:

> **Words to Know**
> figure of speech
> literal

All her friends agreed that Tamika had a heart of gold.

The actual, or **literal,** meaning of the phrase *heart of gold* is that Tamika's heart was made of gold. You know that her heart could not really be made of gold. *Heart of gold* is a **figure of speech**.

A figure of speech has a special meaning when the words are put together. To find the meaning of a figure of speech, do the following:

○ Look carefully at the figure of speech itself.

○ Look at the words and phrases that come before and after it. They may give clues about what the figure of speech means.

All her friends agreed that Tamika had a heart of gold. She never said "no" when someone asked for her help.

The words after the figure of speech tell you that Tamika was kind and helpful. "Tamika had a heart of gold" means that Tamika was very kind.

Understanding figures of speech can help you understand what you read and hear more fully.

Guided Instruction

When you read figures of speech, think about the words or phrases that give clues about their meaning.

Mountain Sunrise

I had never been an early bird, but I woke up at the crack of dawn. I got up, slipped out of the tent, and walked to the top of the hill. The sky was still dark, but at the edge of the distant mountains, I could see a golden glow. I took a seat on a rock and waited.

The glow grew brighter, and I heard birds begin to sing. Soon they made a real racket. All at once I could see the edge of the sun over the mountaintop. Light flooded the mountains. In an instant, the sun was up.

Guided Questions

What is the very first figure of speech you find in the passage?

_____

What does this figure of speech mean?

_____

_____

_____

What clue helps you understand what this figure of speech means?

_____

_____

_____

_____

Answer the questions about the passage.

1. Think about what time of day it is. What does the figure of speech "crack of dawn" mean?

_____

2. Think about what the narrator is doing. What is the meaning of "took a seat"?

_____

3. Think about how the birds sounded. What does "made a racket" mean?

_____

 On Your Own

Discuss

Read the story. Talk with a partner about the underlined figures of speech and what each one means. Then work with your partner to fill in the chart.

Yumi's Tryout

Yumi stood on the stage, her <u>heart hammering</u>. She was alone up there, and the people watching her seemed very far away. The words she had memorized for her tryout were gone, and she felt completely <u>tongue-tied</u>. She had been practicing her part <u>around the clock</u>, but now she had forgotten it all.

"All right," Ms. Munoz called, "you can begin at any time."

<u>Time crawled</u> as Yumi stood silently. She could feel her face turn red, and she was afraid she would <u>burst into tears</u>. _Speak up!_ she told herself.

The words <u>rang a bell</u>, and suddenly the lines were <u>on the tip of her</u> tongue. "Speak up, Father!" she began, and <u>before she knew it</u>, she was done.

"Thank you, Yumi, that was <u>first-rate</u>!" Ms. Munoz said. "We will let everyone know what parts they have in the play by tomorrow."

Figure of Speech	Meaning
heart hammering	
tongue-tied	
speak up	

Complete these activities based on the passage you just read.

1 Which phrase is a figure of speech?

   A "She was alone"

   B "burst into tears"

   C "Yumi stood silently"

   D "she remembered everything"

2 The phrase "the words rang a bell" means that

   A someone was playing a bell.

   B Yumi's voice sounded like a bell.

   C the words sounded like a bell.

   D the words reminded Yumi of something.

3 The phrase "on the tip of her tongue" means

_____

4 When Ms. Munoz says Yumi's tryout was "first-rate," she means that

_____

Writing Connection

5 There are three figures of speech in the story that refer to time. On a separate sheet of paper, write the figures of speech and explain what they mean.

A Social-Network Profile

Media Connection

Choose a partner who likes the same books you like. Decide on a favorite character from one of the books. Then think about your character: How old is he or she? What does he or she look like? What kinds of movies, books, and songs does the character like?

With your partner, create an online profile for the character you have chosen for a social networking Web site. Look at the information the site asks for and write a profile for the character that could go on the site.

The Moral of the Story Is...

Literature Connection

The Greek writer Aesop wrote many fables about animals. Each fable has a moral that Aesop wrote down. The moral expresses the fable's theme.

With a partner, look online at a selection of Aesop's fables. Choose one with a moral that you think would be useful in your own life. Print out or copy the fable. With your partner, make a poster with the moral on it. You can illustrate the poster. Then read the fable aloud to the class, holding up the poster. Speak clearly and distinctly. Afterward, discuss what the morals in all the posters have in common.

A Retelling Without Words

Music/Arts Connection

Work with a small group. Choose a story you have all read that you think could be retold as a wordless comic book. Follow these steps to retell your story:

- Decide how many illustrations you will have in your retelling.

- Choose an event from the story to show in each illustration.

- Decide who will draw or paint each illustration in the retelling.

- Collect all the illustrations and put them in order.

Be sure each frame of your comic book clearly shows the event that happens. If possible, incorporate your comic book into a computer slide presentation to display to the class. You can also show them the hard copy of the comic book. Encourage them to figure out what happens in the story.

Staging a Book

Collaborative Learning

With a small group, choose a chapter of a book you have all read to act out. These steps will help you get ready to perform your scene:

○ Choose a director to be in charge.

○ Decide who will play each character in the scene.

○ Write the dialogue for each character.

○ Work together to rehearse the scene. If possible, find props and costumes that will work in the scene. Remember to speak at an appropriate pace.

○ Perform the scene for your class or a larger group. If you can, have a friend videotape your performance.

Lesson 21

Identifying Main Ideas

RI.3.2	Determine the main idea of a text; recount the key details and explain how they support the main idea.
CCR.R.2	Determine central ideas or themes of a text and analyze their development; summarize the key supporting details and ideas.
CCR.W.9	Draw evidence from literary or informational texts to support analysis, reflection, and research.

 ## Understand the Standards

A **main idea** is the overall point of a paragraph. It can be summed up in a sentence. Sometimes the sentence is explicitly stated in the paragraph.

Details are the points in the paragraph that support or explain the main idea. They **connect** the ideas to the main idea.

Writers use **details** to support or clarify the main idea of a paragraph. Readers learn to identify the main idea and the details to understand what the writer is saying.

> **Words to Know**
> main idea
> details
> connect

 ## Guided Instruction

Imagine that you are reading an article in a magazine. You come across this paragraph:

Prairie Dogs

History Connection

Prairie dogs are small animals that lived on the Great Plains of the United States. Once there were billions of them. But by the early 1900s, only a fraction were left. Ranchers shot or poisoned them to clear land for cattle grazing. Sometimes diseases raged through their colonies. Today prairie dog "towns" are protected in places like Yellowstone National Park. You can watch prairie dogs guarding their burrows from predators.

Guided Questions

What is the "big idea" that the entire paragraph is about?

_____

_____

There are several ideas about prairie dogs in the paragraph. You can make a list of some of the important ones.

Examples:

Once there were billions of them.

Prairie dogs are small animals that lived on the Great Plains of the United States.

Today prairie dog "towns" are protected in places like Yellowstone National Park.

Which of these ideas is more important than the others? If you were making an outline, which would be the topic at the top of the outline?

Label each of the following sentences from the paragraph *main idea* or *detail*.

1. Prairie dogs are small animals that lived on the Great Plains of the United States.

_____

2. Once there were billions of them.

_____

3. Ranchers shot or poisoned them to clear land for cattle grazing.

_____

4. You can watch prairie dogs guarding their burrows from predators.

_____

On Your Own

Discuss

Science Connection

Read the passage. Draw a line under the sentence that states the main idea. List three sentences with details that support the main idea. Work with a partner to discuss your choices.

River otters are playful acrobats of the water. They are like long, slim weasels that swim. Otters have long tails. Their tails are nearly one-third the length of their bodies. Their tails help them leap, flip, and dive after fish. They live in burrows alongside rivers, lakes, or streams.

main idea sentence

detail sentences

Answer the questions below.

1 Which of the following is a main idea sentence?

   A Ice cream flavors can range from plain vanilla to hot cherry flamingo.

   B The challenge is to eat one before it drips all over you!

   C My favorite food is an ice cream cone.

   D The cone can be waffle or sugar.

2 Read the sentence below.

   My least favorite animal to meet on a hike is a bear.

   Which sentence would not be a detail for this main idea?

   A Snakes have slithered across my trail.

   B I have watched a skunk walk quietly through the woods.

   C Chipmunks noisily scold me as I pass.

   D My cat curls up in my lap to watch TV with me.

3 What would be a good main idea sentence for this detail?

   The beaver uses its tail to build its home.

   _____

   _____

4 What would be a good detail sentence for this main idea?

   Animals are fascinating to watch.

   _____

   _____

Writing Connection

5 Now it's your turn. On your own sheet of paper, write a paragraph that has a main idea sentence and at least three detail sentences. Underline your main idea sentence.

 Measuring Up® to the Common Core

RI.3.1	Ask and answer questions to demonstrate understanding of a text, referring explicitly to the text as the basis for the answers.
RI.3.2	Determine the main idea of a text; recount the key details and explain how they support the main idea.
CCR.R.1	Read closely to determine what the text says explicitly and to make logical inferences from it; cite specific textual evidence when writing or speaking to support conclusions drawn from the text.
CCR.R.2	Determine central ideas or themes of a text and analyze their development; summarize the key supporting details and ideas.

Understand the Standards

Readers ask questions as they read. They are listening to the author's voice and responding to the conversation. If they are "listening" well, readers should be able to answer the questions they ask.

Words to Know
theme
inference
summary

A **theme** is the general purpose or point of a piece of writing.

An **inference** is an idea that is suggested but not explicitly stated.

A **summary** is a few brief sentences stating what the paragraph is saying.

Guided Instruction

Suppose you are reading an article in a magazine. You read the following.

History Connection

Saving Sequoias

Guided Questions

The first step toward creating a national park was taken back in 1855. That's when Galen Clark saw his first giant sequoia. Clark was among the thousands of people who were pouring into California in 1848. The discovery of gold had unleashed a boom of construction. But by 1853 Clark found he had a serious lung problem. Doctors told him he had only six months to live. He decided to spend his final days in the wilderness and headed into the Sierra Nevadas.

There he fell in love with a tree! Not just one tree, but a whole grove of them. His group of Giant Sequoias was called the Mariposa Grove.

What do you think a national park is?

_____

_____

_____

He knew that the huge, beautiful trees would need protection from all the development in Northern California. He and others brought this cause to the U.S. government.

In 1864 President Lincoln signed the Yosemite Grant, which put Clark's Mariposa Grove and Yosemite Valley under protection. Clark stayed on as guardian of the trees. He not only regained his health but also lived to be 96!

Guided Questions

What questions might you ask about Galen Clark and "Saving the Sequoias"?

_____

_____

_____

_____

_____

_____

Here are some examples of questions a reader might ask. Answer these questions. Refer back to the passage as needed.

1. Why did the Mariposa Grove need to be protected?

_____

_____

_____

2. What is a theme of the paragraph?

_____

_____

_____

3. How would you summarize the paragraph?

_____

_____

_____

On Your Own

Ask some questions about the passage below. Write each question in its own box in the Question column. Work with a partner to answer the questions. Write your answers in the Answer column next to each question. Then use the answers to write a summary of the paragraph.

History
Connection

Saving Yosemite

Perhaps the most important person to continue Galen Clark's work was John Muir. From his first visit to Yosemite Valley in 1878, Muir felt he had found a very special place. Muir worked tirelessly to have Yosemite preserved, as Yellowstone National Park had been in 1872. But it wasn't until 1906 that Muir would persuade President Theodore Roosevelt to preserve Yosemite.

Question	Answer
Summary	

Complete these activities based on the passage you just read.

1 What can you infer about Clark and Muir from the passage?

   A Both were young, healthy men.

   B Each found a special place he wanted to preserve.

   C Both wanted to create a national park.

   D Each had come to California to search for gold.

2 Which sentence states a theme of the passage about John Muir?

   A Muir came to Yosemite to meet Galen Clark.

   B John Muir created the nation's first national park.

   C Muir's work greatly expanded Clark's achievements.

   D Clark could not have succeeded without John Muir.

3 What does it mean to preserve something?

   _____

4 Read the statement below.

   Galen Clark should be considered the father of national parks.

   In your own words, tell whether this statement is supported by the passages.

   _____

   _____

**Writing
Connection**

5 You can infer from the paragraphs that Galen Clark and John Muir had some common interests. On your own sheet of paper, summarize what these common interests were.

RI.3.5   Use text features and search tools to locate information relevant to a given topic efficiently.
CCR.R.5   Analyze the structure of texts, including how specific sentences, paragraphs, and larger portions of the text relate to each other and the whole.

 Understand the Standards

Writers organize topics according to a plan, or **structure**. One kind of structure is time sequence, or chronological order. Another structure is cause and effect. Still another structure is comparison and contrast. These structures can help you **locate**, or find, information in a passage.

> **Words to Know**
> structure
> locate

○ **Chronological order** sometimes uses ordering words such as *first, next,* and *last.* Dates can also be used to show time order:

in the 1950s → in 1962 → in 1973

○ **Cause and effect** shows that something is the result of an earlier action.

Rachel Carson writes about pesticides. → DDT is banned.

 Guided Instruction

You might find the following paragraphs in a science magazine or textbook. Look at how the passage is organized. Read the passage and complete the activities.

Rachel Carson and *Silent Spring*

Science Connection

Have you ever watched a bald eagle soaring across a blue sky? This magnificent bird almost disappeared from our skies. There were fewer than 500 nesting pairs in the 1950s. In 1962 Rachel Carson published the results of studies she and other scientists had made. These studies showed harmful effects of pesticides. Farmers were using chemicals to kill insects that could eat their crops. Carson's study found that the shells of the eggs of many birds, including eagles, were becoming too thin to protect the babies inside. One cause was a buildup of the pesticide DDT in the birds' systems. DDT would collect in fish. Then it would collect in eagles and other animals that ate the fish.

Guided Questions

What clues in the passage make you suspect the writer is using time order to organize the passage?

_____

_____

_____

Carson's book *Silent Spring* was attacked by farmers and chemical companies. But eventually people saw that her arguments were valid. A ban on DDT was enacted in 1973. Other people began studying different ways chemicals were harming the environment. The environmental movement grew from these studies. The Environmental Protection Agency was created. Soon the great eagles began to make a comeback to the skies.

Guided Questions

Is DDT a cause or an effect? Why?

_____

_____

_____

When you read, look for the organizational structures of a piece of writing. You can follow actions in chronological order. You can also follow causes and effects.

Examples: There were fewer than 500 nesting pairs in the 1950s. . . . Soon the great eagles began to make a comeback to the skies.

Think: If there were only about 1,000 eagles at one time, something must have changed to have them make a comeback. The writer says that Rachel Carson's work helped to make it happen. So her writing would be a cause of the eagles' comeback.

Try these examples yourself. Identify how each sentence shows a cause and an effect.

1. DDT would collect in fish. Then it would collect in eagles and other animals that ate the fish.

   _____

   _____

2. A ban on DDT was enacted in 1973. . . . Soon the great eagles began to make a comeback to the skies.

   _____

   _____

3. In 1962 Rachel Carson published the results of studies she and other scientists had made. . . . Carson's book *Silent Spring* was attacked by farmers and chemical companies.

   _____

   _____

On Your Own

Collaborative Learning

Refer to the science magazine paragraphs as paragraph 1 and paragraph 2. Locate each of the following ideas and tell which paragraph it came from. Work with a partner to identify the paragraphs. Look for key words to find the information you seek. Complete the following activities. Refer back to the passage as needed.

1 A. Carson's book was titled *Silent Spring*. _____

B. There were fewer than 500 nesting pairs of eagles in the 1950s. _____

C. The environmental movement grew from studies of how pesticides and other chemicals were harming the environment. _____

D. The shells of the eggs of birds, including eagles, were becoming too thin to protect the babies inside. _____

Answer the questions based on the passage.

2 Which of the following happened last?

A The Environmental Protection Agency was created.

B Rachel Carson's book *Silent Spring* was published.

C Fewer than 500 nesting pairs of eagles were to be found.

D The pesticide DDT was banned.

3 Read the sentence below.

DDT was building up in birds and other animals.

Which sentence describes a cause of this situation?

A Rachel Carson published *Silent Spring*.

B The Environmental Protection Agency was created.

C People were studying the effects of pesticides on the environment.

D Farmers were spraying pesticides on their crops.

4 What kind of structure is chronological order?

5 Read the sentence below.

The Environmental Protection Agency was created.

Tell in your own words what the causes are for this effect.

_____

_____

_____

_____

6 Sometimes causes can also be effects, and effects can also be causes. On your own sheet of paper, explain how this event is both a cause and an effect:

Rachel Carson publishes *Silent Spring*.

RI.3.3	Describe the relationship between a series of historical events, scientific ideas or concepts, or steps in technical procedures in a text, using language that pertains to time, sequence, and cause/effect.
RI.3.8	Describe the logical connection between particular sentences and paragraphs in a text.
SL.3.1	Engage effectively in a range of collaborative discussions with diverse partners on grade 3 topics and texts, building on others' ideas and expressing their own clearly.
	a. Come to discussions prepared, having read or studied required material; explicitly draw on that preparation and other information known about the topic to explore ideas under discussion.
	b. Follow agreed-upon rules for discussions (e.g., gaining the floor in respectful ways, listening to others with care, speaking one at a time about the topics and texts under discussion).
	c. Ask questions to check understanding of information presented, stay on topic, and link their comments to the remarks of others.
	d. Explain their own ideas and understanding in light of the discussion.
CCR.R.3	Analyze how and why individuals, events, and ideas develop and interact over the course of the text.
CCR.R.5	Analyze the structure of texts, including how specific sentences, paragraphs, and larger portions of the text relate to each other and the whole.
CCR.R.8	Delineate and evaluate the argument and specific claims in a text, including the validity of the reasoning as well as the relevance and sufficiency of the evidence.
CCR.W.9	Draw evidence from literary or informational texts to support analysis, reflection, and research.

Understand the Standards

One way to follow an article is to make a **time line**, or ordered list, of the key events the writer includes. Then you can see the **sequence**, or time order, of events. You can also see the **logical connections** the writer used in presenting the information. You may find comparisons, cause-and-effect relationships, or other useful ways to present information.

Words to Know
time line
sequence
logical connections

For passages about historical events, you may also want to look at a map to find the places mentioned. That way you can follow the activities the writer describes.

Guided Instruction

You might find an article like this in a history book:

History Connection

Lewis and Clark

Two years of travel and exploration changed the face of the United States forever. In 1803, President Thomas Jefferson purchased the Louisiana Territory from France. He charged two men to explore this vast, uncharted territory. On May 14, 1804, Meriwether Lewis and William Clark set out. They started at the Mississippi River near St. Louis. They traveled up the Missouri River. By October they reached the villages

Guided Questions

How does the opening sentence suggest what to read for?

_____

_____

of the Mandans/Hidatsas and stopped for the winter. By December Fort Mandan was built across the river from the main village.

In April 1805, they left the fort, near today's Bismarck, North Dakota, to resume their trek. They were now led by a French-Canadian fur trader and his wife, Sacajawea, a Shoshone Indian. Sacajawea's knowledge of the ways of Indian tribes and their languages helped the expedition survive. They crossed the Rockies, the most difficult part of their journey. By October they reached what is now the Columbia River and followed it to the Pacific Ocean. They built Fort Clatsop and spent the winter there. In March 1806, they began their return trip.

Guided Questions

When you start to see dates in the text, what do you suspect the writer is doing?

_____

_____

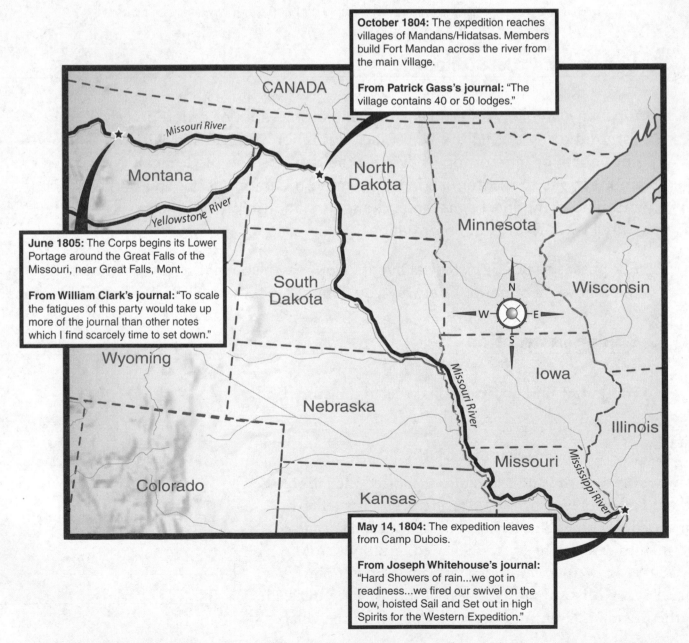

October 1804: The expedition reaches villages of Mandans/Hidatsas. Members build Fort Mandan across the river from the main village.

From Patrick Gass's journal: "The village contains 40 or 50 lodges."

June 1805: The Corps begins its Lower Portage around the Great Falls of the Missouri, near Great Falls, Mont.

From William Clark's journal: "To scale the fatigues of this party would take up more of the journal than other notes which I find scarcely time to set down."

May 14, 1804: The expedition leaves from Camp Dubois.

From Joseph Whitehouse's journal: "Hard Showers of rain...we got in readiness...we fired our swivel on the bow, hoisted Sail and Set out in high Spirits for the Western Expedition."

 Measuring Up® to the Common Core

By September when Lewis and Clark arrived in St. Louis, everyone was amazed. They had been given up for dead. But Lewis and Clark's notes, descriptions, drawings, and tales caused a sensation. Their success inspired many people to head west. As a consequence of the party's reaching the Pacific, the United States claimed the Oregon Territory. The country now reached from the Atlantic to the Pacific.

Guided Questions

Complete the following activities based on the passage you just read.

1. Complete the following time line.

Lewis and Clark Time Line	
Date	Event
1803	Louisiana purchase
May 14, 1804	
October 1804	
December 1804	Fort Mandan (winter camp) completed
April 1805	
May 1805	See Rockies for the first time
June 1805	
September 1805	Finish crossing the Rockies
Winter 1805–1806	Build and live in Fort Clatsop
March 1806	
September 1806	

Look for clues in the text to see which events happened first, and then which ones followed. Then *think* about what you read. Find the connections between the different points on your time line.

Example:

On May 14, 1804, Meriwether Lewis and William Clark set out. . . .

By October they reached the villages of the Mandan/Hidatsas . . .

Think: If they left in May and reached the villages in October, they traveled for about six months before they stopped. That was a lot of territory to cover by traveling up a river! Remember, in those days there were no roads or cars for travel, so the explorers depended on boats to travel up the river.

Now consider these clues from the text. How are the events connected? Describe your thinking.

2. In April, 1805, they left the fort. . . . They crossed the Rockies, the most difficult part of their journey.

Think: _____

_____

_____

3. In March, 1806, they began their return trip. . . . By September when they arrived in St. Louis everyone was amazed.

Think: _____

_____

_____

4. As a consequence of the party's reaching the Pacific . . . The country now reached from the Atlantic to the Pacific.

Think: _____

_____

_____

On Your Own

Discuss

Read these five passages from the article. Work with a partner to put the passages in time order. Which came first, second, third, fourth, and last? Work with a partner to order them in the chart. Then talk with your partner about the logical connections among the passages.

By October they reached what is now the Columbia River and followed it to the Pacific Ocean.

As a consequence of the party's reaching the Pacific, the United States claimed the Oregon Territory.

They were now led by a French-Canadian fur trader and his wife, Sacajawea, a Shoshone Indian.

In 1803, President Thomas Jefferson purchased the Louisiana Territory from France.

By October they reached the Mandan villages and stopped for the winter.

Passage	Number in Time Order

Complete these activities based on the passage you just read.

1 The event that occurred first is

   A arriving at the Mandan villages.

   B building Fort Clatsop.

   C departing from an area near St. Louis.

   D reaching an area near St. Louis with information about the Northwest Territory.

2 Read the sentences below.

> **Two years of travel and exploration changed the face of the United States forever. The country now reached from the Atlantic to the Pacific.**

What is the relationship between these two sentences in the passage?

A main idea and detail

B introduction and conclusion

C cause and effect

D comparison and contrast

3 According to the passage, what helped the expedition to survive?

___

Writing Connection

4 Read this sentence from the passage.

> **But Lewis and Clark's notes, descriptions, drawings, and tales caused a sensation.**

In your own words, tell what effect resulted from this cause.

___

 Elevate **5** The passage describes the explorations of Lewis and Clark. On your own sheet of paper, evaluate how their accomplishments affected the development of the United States. Use evidence from the passage to support your ideas.

Critical Thinking

6 Work with a group of classmates to create a multimedia presentation about a remote place that you would like to explore like Lewis and Clark did. Outside the U.S., it can be as remote as Newfoundland or the Galapagos Islands. Inside the U.S., you might pick Okefenokee Swamp or the Mount St. Helens region in Oregon. Find music, videos, and stories in print that you can combine to tell about the place and why you would like to explore it. Share your presentation with your classmates.

Analyzing Point of View

RI.3.6   Distinguish their own point of view from that of the author of a text.

CCR.R.6   Assess how point of view or purpose shapes the content and style of a text.

CCR.SL.3   Evaluate a speaker's point of view, reasoning, and use of evidence and rhetoric.

 ## Understand the Standards

Point of view is the perspective from which a topic is addressed. Good readers are able to recognize this viewpoint and distinguish it from their own.

> **Words to Know**
> point of view
> opinion
> fact

As a way to help identify the point of view of a writer, it's important to distinguish between the writer's opinions and actual facts.

- An **opinion** is a personal viewpoint on a topic that is not always backed up by facts.

    I think it might rain tomorrow.

- A **fact** is information about a topic that can be verified by more than one source as true.

    It's raining right now.

 ## Guided Instruction

Imagine that you are reading an article in a magazine. You come across this paragraph:

Geography
Connection

Caribou

Caribou herds in Alaska's Arctic National Wildlife Refuge are shrinking in number. The decrease is happening at an alarming rate. Global warming may be a factor. Rising temperatures affect the habitat of these animals. Temperature change affects their food sources. It can also affect their mobility. If the ground is muddy, it's hard for a caribou to run away. Predators like grizzly bears have an easy time catching a bogged-down caribou!

Guided Questions

In the second sentence, what word expresses the writer's opinion, rather than a fact?

_____

_____

_____

_____

_____

_____

The writer of this paragraph has a particular point of view toward the topic. For example, how would a miner or oil prospector view the plight of the declining caribou? Would this viewpoint be the same as that of a native who depends on the caribou for food? Which of these viewpoints is more likely to be similar to the writer's?

Good writers express a clear point of view toward their topic. In order to determine that point of view, it's important to sift the facts from the opinions that the writer expresses.

Try these examples yourself.

1. Caribou herds in Alaska's Arctic National Wildlife Refuge are shrinking in number.

_____

_____

2. Global warming may be a factor.

_____

_____

3. If the ground is muddy, it's hard for a caribou to run away.

_____

4. Predators like grizzly bears have an easy time catching a bogged-down caribou!

_____

_____

On Your Own

Discuss

Read the statements in this list. Talk about the underlined parts. Which are facts? Which are opinions? Work with a partner to fill in the chart.

Science Connection

Sea Ice

- Sea ice in the Arctic <u>may disappear as early as the summer of 2050</u>, according to recent computer projections.
- September of 2012 showed the <u>lowest level of sea ice on record</u>.
- The loss of sea ice in Alaska <u>may doom the polar bear</u>.
- In a warmer climate, <u>polar bears will be competing with grizzlies and other bears</u> for habitat.
- If enough sea ice melts, the Northwest Passage shipping route <u>may become a reality</u>.
- Warming ocean temperatures <u>increase the rate of loss</u> of sea ice.
- Warming temperatures <u>result from increased carbon emissions as well as from natural processes</u>.
- Colder ocean waters from melting sea ice <u>may cool the lower United States</u>.
- Changing climate patterns <u>will harm both people and wildlife</u>.

Facts	Opinions

Complete the following exercises. Use the passage on caribou and the list on sea ice to help you.

1 Which of the following states an opinion?

   A Caribou are in danger of becoming extinct.

   B Caribou are members of the deer family.

   C Caribou herds migrate from the taiga woodland each summer.

   D Caribou have broad feet that help them move over soft ground.

2 Read the sentence below.

> **The Harding Icefield outside Seward, Alaska, lost more than 70 feet in depth between 1960 and 2000.**

Which statement below is not a fact, based on this sentence?

   A The Harding Icefield is located near Seward, Alaska.

   B The Harding Icefield is thinning.

   C The Harding Icefield is smaller today than it was in 1960.

   D The Harding Icefield will be gone by 2015.

3 Whose point of view is happy about the melting sea ice in the Arctic?

_____

_____

4 Read the statement below.

> **Changing climate patterns will harm both people and wildlife.**

In your own words, tell what the point of view is in this statement.

_____

_____

5 Examine the following statement: "The loss of sea ice in the Arctic may doom the polar bear." On your own sheet of paper, explain how this opinion might become a reality. Explain why you agree or disagree.

Lesson 26

Using Illustrations

RI.3.7   Use information gained from illustrations and the words in a text to demonstrate understanding of the text.

CCR.R.7   Integrate and evaluate content presented in diverse media and formats, including visually and quantitatively, as well as in words.

 ## Understand the Standards

Writers use illustrations, photographs, or diagrams to help make descriptions clear. These **illustrations** show what the writer is describing in words.

> **Words to Know**
> illustrations

Science Connection

Science texts often include diagrams or illustrations to show how things work. A writer might use the illustration below to show the parts of the body.

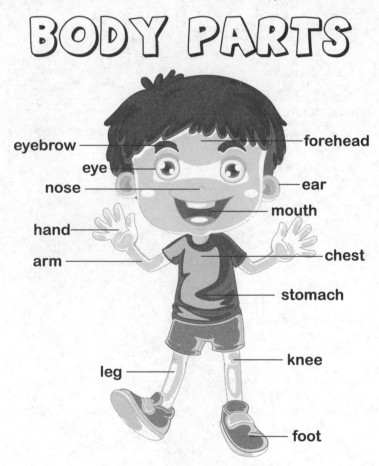

BODY PARTS

eyebrow — forehead
eye
nose — ear
— mouth
hand —
arm — chest
— stomach
— knee
leg —
— foot

Guided Instruction

Read the passage. Study the diagram. Then complete the activities.

Phases of the Moon

Do you ever watch the Moon at night? It seems to change shape night after night. These shapes are called *phases*. The Moon is round, but the phases have different shapes. These shapes result from the Moon orbiting Earth. As the Moon moves in its orbit, we see different views of its reflected light. The four main phases are: new moon (which shows no light), first quarter (which shows the right half of the Moon), full moon (which shows the whole face lit), and third quarter (which shows the left half). There are also crescent shapes between some phases. The crescent shapes change depending on where the Moon is in its 28-day orbit.

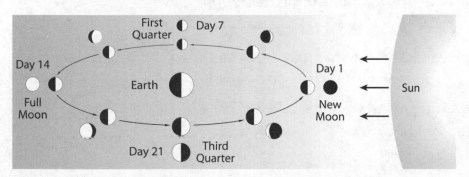

Guided Questions

Why does the writer include a diagram?

_____

_____

In the diagram, why does the new moon appear as just a dark spot in the sky?

_____

_____

_____

_____

_____

Use the illustration to help you answer the following questions.

1. Why does the first quarter moon show the right side of the Moon lit?

_____

_____

2. Why does the full moon show the whole side of the Moon lit?

_____

_____

_____

3. Why does the third quarter moon show the left side of the Moon lit?

_____

_____

_____

On Your Own

Science Connection

Read the following statements. Refer to the illustration of the Moon's phases to evaluate each one. Label each *true* or *false*. Work with a partner to fill in the chart.

1. The full moon occurs at least twice in one orbit around Earth. _____

2. There are two quarter moon phases in the orbit of the Moon around Earth. _____

3. The new moon shows no reflected light toward Earth. _____

4. A crescent moon shape occurs before the first quarter moon phase. _____

5. A crescent moon shape occurs before the third quarter moon phase. _____

6. The crescent moon shape will last more than one night in the Moon's orbit. _____

7. When the shape of the Moon grows larger, it's called *waxing*. The Moon waxes after the third quarter. _____

8. The Moon shines with its own light. _____

True Statements	False Statements

Complete these activities based on the illustration of the Moon's phases.

1 The Moon waxes, or appears larger, after each phase except

  A new moon.

  B first crescent.

  C full moon.

  D first quarter.

2 Read the sentence below.

  The Moon orbits Earth in about 28 days.

  Which of these most likely describes the number of days between the new moon and the full moon?

  A 7 days

  B 14 days

  C 21 days

  D 28 days

3 Describe what makes a full moon.

  _____

  _____

4 Evaluate the statement below.

  The first quarter and third quarter moons look alike.

  In your own words, tell whether this statement is true or not.

  _____

  _____

5 The Moon changes shapes as it orbits Earth. On your own sheet of paper, explain how the Moon moves through its four main phases.

   Measuring Up® to the Common Core

Lesson 27

Comparing and Contrasting Texts

RI.3.9   Compare and contrast the most important points and key details presented in two texts on the same topic.

CCR.R.9   Analyze how two or more texts address similar themes or topics in order to build knowledge or to compare the
             approaches the authors take.

CCR.W.9   Draw evidence from literary or informational texts to support analysis, reflection, and research.

 ## Understand the Standards

Writers usually express their points of view by stating ideas
explicitly. They also choose words that convey an attitude or
feeling toward their topic.

When you read, you **analyze** the statements a writer makes.
Then you compare and contrast statements and ideas.

After you **compare** and **contrast** different ideas, you can **draw conclusions**. Your
conclusions may be different from those of any one writer. But you can explain
your conclusions by referring to a writer's ideas.

> **Words to Know**
> analyze
> compare
> contrast
> draw conclusions

 ## Guided Instruction

These two passages give different points of view on road travel in the
United States:

**Social Studies
Connection**

Highways

The Interstate Highway System began in 1956, under
President Eisenhower. The system's purpose was for national
defense. But travel by interstate soon became a national
pastime. With long stretches between exits, traffic moved
quickly. Eventually, interstate highways came to look a lot
alike. Most have the same hotel chains, restaurants, and gas
stations. So there's a boring regularity from state to state. If
you miss the sign welcoming you to a new state, you might
not even know you left another one behind.

Guided Questions

According to the
first passage, what does
the writer like most about
traveling by interstate?
How can you tell?

_____

_____

Country Roads

Traveling on country roads is the best way to see the United States. Country roads meander over hills and down into valleys. They cross rustic bridges over streams and wind around scenic lakes. Country roads lead to delicious homemade meals at roadside restaurants. Small inns give a homey touch to an overnight stay. Country roads invite you to linger and savor a place. Interstate highways may get you from one place to another faster. But country roads are much more satisfying.

Guided Questions

In the same passage, the writer states, "So there's a boring regularity from state to state." What does it tell you about the writer's attitude toward the topic?

_____

_____

_____

_____

_____

_____

Read these statements from the passages. Explain what each tells you about the writer's attitude.

1. If you miss the sign welcoming you to a new state, you might not know you left another one behind.

_____

_____

2. Country roads lead to delicious homemade meals at roadside restaurants.

_____

_____

3. Country roads invite you to linger and savor a place.

_____

_____

4. Interstate highways may get you from one place to another faster. But country roads are much more satisfying.

_____

_____

 On Your Own

Discuss

Read these sentences from the two passages at the start of this lesson. Think about the underlined phrases. What attitude toward the topic does each one suggest? Work with a partner to explain your analysis. Then, draw a conclusion about the kind of road you prefer. Tell why.

But travel by interstate <u>soon became a national pastime</u>.

With long stretches between exits, traffic <u>moved quickly</u>.

Eventually, interstate highways came to <u>look a lot alike</u>.

Country roads lead to <u>delicious homemade</u> meals at roadside restaurants.

Country roads invite you to <u>linger and savor</u> a place.

But country roads are much <u>more satisfying</u>.

Phrase	Explanation
soon became a national pastime	
moved quickly	
look a lot alike	
delicious homemade	
linger and savor	
more satisfying	

Conclusions

Complete these activities based on the passages at the start of this lesson.

1 The writers of both paragraphs agree on which statement?

   A Country roads are the best way to see the United States.

   B Interstates get you from one place to another faster.

   C Interstates have a boring regularity from state to state.

   D Country roads meander over hills and down into valleys.

2 Read the sentence below.

   They "let you linger and savor a place."

   Which of these does this sentence describe?

   A roads built for national defense

   B interstate highways

   C country roads

   D hotels, restaurants, and gas stations

3 What are the two different points of view suggested by the paragraphs?

   _____

   _____

 Measuring Up® to the Common Core

4 Read the description below.

   Small inns give a homey touch to an overnight stay.

   In your own words, tell what this description suggests.

   _____

   _____

**Writing
Connection**

5 The two passages at the start of this lesson describe different ways to travel by automobile in the United States.

   On a sheet of paper, compare and contrast the two ways. Tell which you prefer and why.

RI.3.4	Determine the meaning of general academic and domain-specific words or phrases in a text relevant to a grade 3 topic or subject area.
SL.3.1	Engage effectively in a range of collaborative discussions with diverse partners on grade 3 topics and texts, building on others' ideas and expressing their own clearly.
	a. Come to discussions prepared, having read or studied required material; explicitly draw on that preparation and other information known about the topic to explore ideas under discussion.
	b. Follow agreed-upon rules for discussions (e.g., gaining the floor in respectful ways, listening to others with care, speaking one at a time about the topics and texts under discussion).
	c. Ask questions to check understanding of information presented, stay on topic, and link their comments to the remarks of others.
	d. Explain their own ideas and understanding in light of the discussion.
CCR.R.4	Interpret words and phrases as they are used in a text, including determining technical, connotative, and figurative meanings, and analyze how specific word choices shape meaning or tone.
CCR.SL.1	Prepare for and participate effectively in a range of conversations and collaborations with diverse partners, building on others' ideas and expressing their own clearly and persuasively.
L.3.3	Use knowledge of language and its conventions when writing, speaking, reading, or listening.
	a. Choose words and phrases for effect.

Understand the Standards

The more you read, the more you will find that no matter how many words you know, you will always encounter new words you do not know. Of course, you can look the new words up in a dictionary, but often you can use context clues and what you already know to figure out their meaning.

A **context clue** is a word or phrase that gives a synonym or description of a term so that the meaning can be inferred. The **connotation** of a word is the meaning suggested by the word in addition to its literal definition.

Words to Know

context clue

connotation

Guided Instruction

Imagine that you are reading a magazine for science class. You come across this paragraph:

Science Connection

The Cardinal

The bright red bird of the woodlands is the cardinal. His crested head makes him look proud and regal. His short, strong beak is perfect for cracking the seeds he loves to eat. If you imitate his distinctive whistle, he will call back to you. The cardinal's mate is quietly pretty. She has touches of red only on her wings, crest, and tail. Cardinals can be found from Canada, south into Texas and Mexico. They do not migrate; they stay in the same area throughout the year.

Guided Questions

What clues do you find for the meaning of *migrate*?

_____

_____

_____

_____

_____

The male will make a flashy entrance at your feeder on a snowy morning. His mate joins him, too, for seeds to see them through a cold winter.

Are the connotations of the words used to describe the cardinal good or bad?

_____

_____

_____

_____

The writer uses description in this paragraph to paint a picture of a particular bird. Some of the words may be unfamiliar, but the context gives clues to their meaning. For example, what kind of head is a "crested" head? What is a cardinal's "whistle"? What does "migrate" mean? What is meant by a "flashy entrance"?

Look for the clues in the context around these words to figure out what they mean. For example, the "crested head" makes the bird appear "proud and regal," so a crest must be some kind of feathery crown.

Try these examples yourself.

1. If you imitate his <u>distinctive whistle</u>, he will call back to you.

_____

_____

_____

2. The male will make a <u>flashy entrance</u> at your feeder on a snowy morning.

_____

_____

_____

3. The cardinal's mate is <u>quietly pretty</u>.

_____

_____

_____

On Your Own

Discuss Read the passage. Talk about the underlined terms. What context clues suggest the meaning for each one? Work with a partner to fill in the chart. Using context clues, give a synonym or definition for each term. Discuss and defend your own ideas before agreeing on a final definition.

Birds

Many birds are easily recognized. The robin is a medium-sized songbird with a red breast. Robins <u>peck</u> worms and bugs from the ground. A smaller bird is the black-<u>capped</u> chikadee. This fluffy black, gray, and white bird <u>chirps</u> a *chika dee dee dee* song. An even smaller bird is the ruby-<u>throated</u> hummingbird. This tiny bird <u>darts</u> into flowers, feeding on <u>nectar</u>. It will also sip sugar water from a feeder.

If you visit a lake or the ocean, you may see a nest of ospreys in a tall treetop. These large, dark brown and white birds feed on fish. They have a <u>wingspan</u> up to six feet. Another easily recognized <u>bird of prey</u> is the red-tailed hawk, with its <u>shrill</u>, <u>piercing</u> cry. And the blue-gray peregrine falcon <u>dives</u> after its <u>prey</u> at speeds over 200 miles per hour!

Term	Context Clues; Definition
peck	
capped	
chirps	
throated	
darts	
nectar	
wingspan	
bird of prey	
shrill, piercing	
dives	
prey	

 Measuring Up® to the Common Core

Complete these activities based on the passage in On Your Own.

1 The chikadee is named for its

A habitat.

B food.

C color.

D song.

2 Read the sentence below.

This tiny bird darts into flowers, feeding on nectar.

Which is the best synonym for *darts*?

A flies

B swims

C zips

D lolls

3 What does it mean to have a "wingspan of up to six feet"?

_____

_____

4 Read the sentence below.

Ospreys, red-tailed hawks, and peregrine falcons are birds of prey.

In your own words, tell what this means.

_____

_____

5 The passage describes the ruby-throated hummingbird "darting" into flowers for nectar, and the peregrine falcon as "diving" after prey at speeds over 200 miles per hour. On your own sheet of paper, explain how darting and diving are similar and different. Then work with a small group. Agree on a list of other living creatures that also dart or dive. Include an interesting detail you find in a book or online about at least two of them.

Main Ideas

Discuss

Work with a partner to select an article that interests you from a magazine or newspaper. Read it together with your partner. Then prepare a list of questions about the main idea and details of the article. Using the text of the article, write answers to the questions on your list. Conclude your project by writing a brief summary of the article.

Past Events

Social Studies Connection

Working in a small group, select a topic from your social studies textbook that interests you. Focus on a chapter of the book that talks about this topic. Make a list of the key points of the chapter. Include the major events of the chapter and the people who played an important role.

When you have completed your list, fill in the important details. Then use your list to make an oral panel presentation of the events of the chapter to your class. Invite questions afterward and answer the questions as fully as possible.

Opposing Viewpoints

Media Connection

Select an article from the op-ed section of an online newspaper or news magazine for kids. It can be an editorial or a letter to the editor. Work with a partner to summarize the writer's point of view on the topic. Then prepare an opposing view of the ideas the writer presented. Be sure to support your position with facts as well as opinions that show your point of view. Then, present the two viewpoints as a debate before your classmates. Finish your debate by summarizing each of the two points of view.

Illustrations

Working with a partner, choose a process to explain with the help of a diagram or illustration. For example, you may want to show the orbits of the planets in the solar system, how a volcano works, or how to make lemonade. Look up information on the Web and prepare an illustration. Then, write the text that will explain what is in your illustration. Mount the project on poster board and present the information to your classmates.

Glossary

Choose a poem you like. Work with a partner to read the poem and make a list of words and phrases that are important to the meaning of the poem. Prepare a glossary that lists the meaning of these words or phrases as they are used in the poem. Be sure to include both the literal dictionary definition of the words or phrases and also the connotations of the words in the poem. You may want to illustrate your glossary with simple drawings or illustrations cut from a magazine. Present the poem and your glossary in a booklet that you can share with classmates.

Lesson 29

Argument (Opinion) Writing

W.3.1	Write opinion pieces on topics or texts, supporting a point of view with reasons. **a.** Introduce the topic or text they are writing about, state an opinion, and create an organizational structure that lists reasons. **b.** Provide reasons that support the opinion. **c.** Use linking words and phrases to connect opinion and reasons. **d.** Provide a concluding statement or section.
W.3.6	With guidance and support from adults, use technology to produce and publish writing as well as to interact and collaborate with others.
W.3.8	Recall information from experiences or gather information from print and digital sources; take brief notes on sources and sort evidence into provided categories.
W.3.10	Write routinely over extended time frames and shorter time frames for a range of discipline-specific tasks, purposes, and audiences.
CCR.W.1	Write arguments to support claims in an analysis of substantive topics or texts, using valid reasoning and relevant and sufficient evidence.
CCR.W.5	Develop and strengthen writing as needed by planning, revising, editing, rewriting, or trying a new approach.
CCR.W.6	Use technology, including the Internet, to produce and publish writing and to interact and collaborate with others.
CCR.W.7	Conduct short as well as more sustained research projects based on focused questions, demonstrating understanding of the subject under investigation.
CCR.W.8	Gather relevant information from multiple print and digital sources, assess the credibility and accuracy of each source, and integrate the information while avoiding plagiarism.
L.3.3	Use knowledge of language and its conventions when writing, speaking, reading, or listening. **b.** Recognize and observe differences between the conventions of spoken and written standard English.

Understand the Standards

Suppose you go to a movie with a friend. You might not agree about the movie. Your friend might like it. You might dislike it. You can talk to each other. You can explain why you feel the way you do.

> **Words to Know**
> point of view
> opinion
> reason

Music/Arts Connection

That's just what a movie reviewer does. The reviewer watches a movie. Then he or she writes about it for a magazine or newspaper. The reviewer gives an opinion about the movie. That opinion is just the reviewer's point of view. Other people may not agree. The reviewer gives reasons to explain his or her opinion.

> *Dirt Bike Blues* was disappointing. It stars many fine actors. However, the actors don't have a real story to tell.

You can tell how this reviewer feels. You can also tell <u>why</u> the reviewer feels disappointed.

When you write an opinion, you write from your own point of view. You must give reasons to explain why you feel the way you do.

- A **point of view** is a way of looking at or thinking about something.

- An **opinion** is what someone thinks or believes.

    Dirt Bike Blues was disappointing.

○ A **reason** is a statement that explains something.

The actors don't have a real story to tell.

Argument (Opinion) Prompt

Writing Connection

> Your class has money for only one field trip this year. Your teacher wants the class to choose between visiting the zoo and visiting a battlefield and history museum. Your job is to convince the class that your choice is better. Write a paragraph that states your opinion. Give clear reasons for your choice.

Planning

Purpose and Audience

Whenever you write, you must think: Why am I writing? Who will read my work? The answer to the first question is your purpose. The answer to the second question is your audience.

Use the prompt to answer these questions.

1. Why are you writing a paragraph?

_____

2. Who will read your paragraph?

_____

Prewriting

When you write an opinion, you start with your opinion. You follow your opinion with reasons that support it.

For this prompt, the first thing you must do is make a choice. That is your point of view.

What two choices are you given in the prompt? Write them here.

_____   _____

Circle the choice you like better.

     Measuring Up® to the Common Core

Now you have enough information to write your opinion.
Write it in the box here.

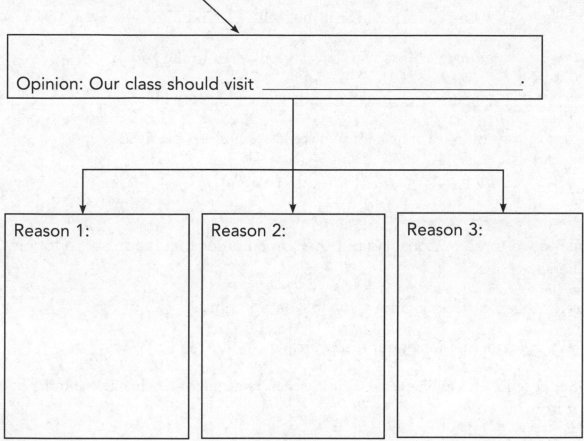

Opinion: Our class should visit _____ .

Reason 1:

Reason 2:

Reason 3:

Why did you make that choice? Write your reasons in the boxes above.

Drafting

Organizing

Make choices as you write. Begin with a topic sentence that states your opinion.
Put your reasons in an order that makes sense to you. You may want to put them
in order from most to least important.

Here is Jonah's answer to the prompt.

> Our class should visit the battlefield and history museum. Most of us have already been to the zoo. It might seem boring. A battlefield and history museum could teach us a lot. We could see how people lived long ago.

Jonah gave three reasons. He put them in an order that made sense for his audience.

Answer these questions about Jonah's paragraph.

1. Which reason did Jonah put first? Circle it.

2. Suppose Jonah's audience were his teacher. How might he change the order of reasons?

Linking Words and Phrases

You can use many different words to connect your ideas. This box shows some examples.

| because | for example | since | therefore |

Look at this version of Jonah's paragraph.

> Our class should visit the battlefield and history museum. Since most of us have already been to the zoo, it might seem boring. A battlefield and history museum could teach us a lot. For example, we could see how people lived long ago.

Answer these questions about the new version of Jonah's paragraph.

1. What word did Jonah use to connect these two sentences?
Most of us have already been to the zoo. It might seem boring.

_____

2. What words did Jonah add to his last sentence? How do they connect the last sentence to the one that came before?

_____

_____

Revising and Editing

Revising for Content and Argument

After you write, read your work. Have a classmate or an adult read it, too. Use this checklist to see what you might fix.

REVISING AN OPINION
❏ Can the reader tell what my opinion is?
❏ Can I add words to make my opinion stronger?
❏ Are my reasons strong and convincing?

Read Jonah's changes.

> definitely
> Our class should visit the battlefield and history
>   ∧
>
> museum. Since most of us have already been to the
>   childish and
> zoo, it might seem boring. A battlefield and history
>   ∧
>
> museum could teach us a lot. For example, we could
>
> see how people lived long ago.

Answer these questions about the edited version of Jonah's paragraph.

1. What word did Jonah add to make his opinion stronger?

_____

2. What words did Jonah add to make his reasons more convincing? How would that help to convince his audience?

_____

Revising for Clarity and Style

You can revise your work to make it clearer for your reader. You can change things to make your writing sound "more like you." You can make sure the words you use are right for your audience.

Jonah is happy with the order of his reasons. He thinks that his paragraph has a clear topic sentence. He feels that his words fit his audience.

REVISING AN OPINION

❏ Does my opinion have a clear topic sentence?

❏ Are my reasons in an order that makes sense?

❏ Did I use words that fit my audience?

Do you agree with Jonah? Tell what you think of his paragraph. Give reasons for your opinion.

_____

_____

_____

Proofreading

Before you finish writing, look for mistakes using the checklist to the right.

<table>
<tr><td>

PROOFREADING CHECKLIST

❏ Did I indent my paragraphs?

❏ Did I use capital letters correctly?

❏ Did I use punctuation marks correctly?

❏ Did I spell all words correctly?

</td></tr>
</table>

Yoshi wrote and edited this opinion. Use the proofreading marks in Appendix 2 to proofread Yoshi's paragraph.

> I think are class should go to the zoo. First, maya the elephant just had a baby, and we can see it. Second we can see the new penguin show. Last, the drive to the zoo is so beautiful Therefore, I hope you agree that we should vizit the zoo.

Publishing

When you publish your writing, you share it with the public. The public is your audience.

A movie reviewer publishes opinion writing in a newspaper or magazine. Jonah and Yoshi wrote paragraphs to convince their classmates. How will they share their opinions?

This is what they decided to do.

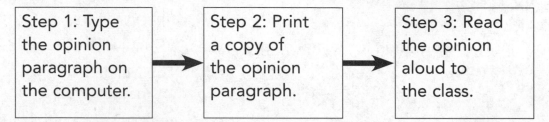

Step 1: Type the opinion paragraph on the computer. → Step 2: Print a copy of the opinion paragraph. → Step 3: Read the opinion aloud to the class.

Try it yourself. One person can read Jonah's paragraph aloud. The other can read Yoshi's paragraph aloud. Which one convinces your class? Why?

Our class should definitely visit the battlefield and history museum. Since most of us have already been to the zoo, it might seem childish and boring. A battlefield and history museum could teach us a lot. For example, we could see how people lived long ago. by Jonah	I think our class should go to the zoo. First, Maya the elephant just had a baby, and we can see it. Second, we can see the new penguin show. Last, the drive to the zoo is so beautiful! Therefore, I hope you agree that we should visit the zoo. by Yoshi

On Your Own

 Choose one of these prompts. Write your own opinion paragraph. Follow the steps in this lesson.

A REVIEW	A RESPONSE
1. Read one of the passages in Chapter 3 of this book. Did you like it? Imagine that you are writing about it for your school magazine. Give your opinion of the passage. Tell what you liked or disliked. Explain why.	**2.** A famous scientist, Albert Einstein, once said: "Imagination is more important than knowledge." Was he right? Decide for yourself. Explain your point of view to your teacher. Give three reasons why you agree or disagree with Albert Einstein.
A LETTER TO A FRIEND	**A LETTER TO THE PRINCIPAL**
3. Your friend is thinking about dropping soccer and playing ice hockey instead. He wonders if this is the right thing to do. Write your friend a letter. Tell him your opinion. Be sure to include some convincing reasons so that he will agree with you.	**4.** The school is building a new playground. The principal wants to know what to include in the playground. Think of one thing you would like to see in a new playground. Write a letter to your principal. Tell your principal what you would like to see. Start with a topic sentence. Add reasons that will convince your principal.

Lesson 30

Informative/Explanatory Writing

W.3.2	Write informative/explanatory texts to examine a topic and convey ideas and information clearly. **a.** Introduce a topic and group related information together; include illustrations when useful to aiding comprehension. **b.** Develop the topic with facts, definitions, and details. **c.** Use linking words and phrases to connect ideas within categories of information. **d.** Provide a concluding statement or section.
W.3.6	With guidance and support from adults, use technology to produce and publish writing as well as to interact and collaborate with others.
W.3.7	Conduct short research projects that build knowledge about a topic.
CCR.W.2	Write informative/explanatory texts to examine and convey complex ideas and information clearly and accurately through the effective selection, organization, and analysis of content.
CCR.W.5	Develop and strengthen writing as needed by planning, revising, editing, rewriting, or trying a new approach.
CCR.W.6	Use technology, including the Internet, to produce and publish writing and to interact and collaborate with others.
CCR.W.8	Gather relevant information from multiple print and digital sources, assess the credibility and accuracy of each source, and integrate the information while avoiding plagiarism.
RI.3.10	By the end of the year, read and comprehend informational texts, including history/social studies, science, and technical texts, at the high end of the grades 2–3 text complexity band independently and proficiently.
L.3.3	Use knowledge of language and its conventions when writing, speaking, reading, or listening. **a.** Choose words and phrases for effect. **b.** Recognize and observe differences between the conventions of spoken and written standard English.

Understand the Standards

Real World Connection

Have you ever looked in an encyclopedia? You can learn facts about everything in the world! Different people wrote those articles. Scientists wrote about science. Dancers wrote about dance.

People write about topics they know. They also write to learn new facts.

For example, you might read this in an encyclopedia.

> The eastern box turtle is a hinge-shelled turtle. It is found in the eastern United States.

This might make you ask some questions. What is a hinge-shelled turtle? Is the eastern box turtle found in Pennsylvania? You would need to look further to get more information.

Words to Know
topic
fact
inform
explain

Writing Connection

You could put together the information you get about turtles in a report.

- A **topic** is the subject of a piece of writing.

- A **fact** is a statement that can be proved or checked.

- When you write to **inform,** you give facts about a topic.

- When you write to **explain,** you tell how something is made or done.

148 English Language Arts — Level C   Copying is illegal.   Measuring Up® to the Common Core

Informative/Explanatory Prompt

Someone has offered to give your school two fainting goats. They will live in the courtyard. No one is sure whether this is a good idea. Your principal wants to know more about this kind of goat. Learn about fainting goats. Write a short report for your principal to read.

Planning

Purpose and Audience

Your purpose is the reason you are writing. Informative/explanatory writing may be done to explain or to give information. Your audience is the person or group that will read your work.

Use the prompt to answer these questions.

1. Why are you writing a report?

_____

2. Who will read your report?

_____

Prewriting

Some writing comes right out of your head. To write a report, you must use outside sources. Where could you find information about fainting goats? Name two places.

_____   _____

Althea took notes about fainting goats. Read her notes.

> ### Notes About Fainting Goats
>
> smaller than most goats   when startled, they tip over
>
> fainting caused by
> a muscle disorder   from 60 to 170 pounds
>
> friendly, easy to care for
>
> about 17 to 25 inches high   eat hay and grain mix

Althea has some good notes. She starts to see how they can fit together in a report.

Help Althea organize her notes. Circle the notes that tell what fainting goats look like. Underline the notes that tell about taking care of fainting goats. Box the notes that tell about their "fainting."

Drafting

Organizing

Once you have notes and have organized them, you are ready to write.

Here is Althea's plan for writing. It is called an outline.

> I. Introduction
>
> II. What Fainting Goats Look Like
>
> III. Taking Care of Fainting Goats
>
> IV. Why Fainting Goats Faint
>
> V. Conclusion

Answer these questions about Althea's plan.

1. Where will Althea tell about what fainting goats eat? _____

2. Where will Althea tell how tall fainting goats get? _____

3. The principal is worried about keeping fainting goats. Which part of Althea's report might be most important to the principal? Why do you think so?

_____

_____

Linking Words and Phrases

You can use many different words to connect your ideas. This box shows some examples.

also	and	another	but	more

This is Part II of Althea's report.

> Fainting goats are smaller than most goats. Small
>
> ones are 17 inches high, and the biggest ones are
>
> around 25 inches high. They can weigh as little as
>
> 60 pounds, but big ones weigh as much as 170 pounds.

Answer these questions about Althea's paragraph.

1. What joining word did Althea use to connect information about the height of fainting goats?

_____

2. What joining word did Althea use to contrast the lightest goats with the heaviest goats?

_____

Revising and Editing

Revising for Content and Argument

After you write, read your work. Have a classmate or an adult read it, too. Use this checklist to see what you might fix.

REVISING INFORMATIVE/ EXPLANATORY WRITING
- ❏ Is my topic clear?
- ❏ Did I use facts, definitions, and details to give information?
- ❏ Did I include any information that is not important?

Read Althea's introduction. Look at the changes she made.

> are small goats that
> Fainting goats are often kept as pets. ~~I once saw one~~
> ~~on a farm when I went to pick berries.~~ The goats are
> friendly and easy to care for.

Answer these questions about Althea's edited paragraph.

1. What words did Althea add to her definition of fainting goats?

_____

2. What sentence did Althea take out? Why?

_____

REVISING INFORMATIVE/ EXPLANATORY WRITING
- ❏ Did I start with an introduction to the topic?
- ❏ Are my facts grouped together in a way that makes sense?
- ❏ Did I end with a conclusion that sums up the main idea?
- ❏ Did I use language that is right for a formal paper?

Revising for Clarity and Style

Revise your writing to make it clear and easy to read.

Read Part IV of Althea's report. Look at the changes she made.

>   Fainting goats ~~don't~~ ^{do not} really faint. When they are
>
> startled, they tip over. A muscle disorder causes this.
>
> ~~They eat hay and grain.~~

Answer these questions about Althea's edited paragraph.

1. Why did Althea change *don't* to *do not*? _____

2. Why did Althea cut the last sentence? _____

Proofreading

Before you finish writing, look for mistakes using the checklist to the right.

Althea wrote and edited her report. Use the proofreading marks in Appendix 2 to proofread Part III of her report.

> PROOFREADING CHECKLIST
>
> ❏ Did I indent my paragraphs?
>
> ❏ Did I use capital letters correctly?
>
> ❏ Did I use punctuation marks correctly?
>
> ❏ Did I spell all words correctly?

>   Farmers says that fainting goats are very easy to
>
> care for. They eat a simple mix of hay and grain.
>
> They are friendly and gentul.

Publishing

When you publish your writing, you share it with your audience.

Encyclopedia writers publish their work online or in a book. Althea wrote a report for her principal. Here is how she decided to share it.

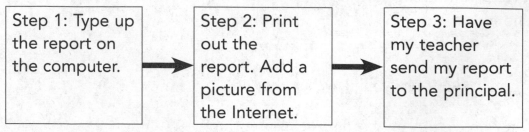

Step 1: Type up the report on the computer. → Step 2: Print out the report. Add a picture from the Internet. → Step 3: Have my teacher send my report to the principal.

Read Althea's whole report. Look online to find a picture that she could add to her report. Tell your class why you chose the picture you did.

> All About Fainting Goats
> by Althea L.
>
> Fainting goats are small goats that are often kept as pets. The goats are friendly and easy to care for.
>
> Fainting goats are smaller than most goats. Small ones are 17 inches high, and the biggest ones are around 25 inches high. They can weigh as little as 60 pounds, but big ones weigh as much as 170 pounds.
>
> Farmers say that fainting goats are very easy to care for. They eat a simple mix of hay and grain. They are friendly and gentle.
>
> Fainting goats do not really faint. When they are startled, they tip over. A muscle disorder causes this.
>
> Fainting goats seem like good pets for a family or for our school. They are small, easygoing, and unusual.

 Measuring Up® to the Common Core

On Your Own

 Choose one of these prompts. Follow the steps in this lesson to do your own informative/explanatory writing.

AN ARTICLE	DIRECTIONS
1. If you were asked to write an article for a kids' encyclopedia, what topic would you choose? Think of a topic you know well. It could be anything from apples to zebras. Write a paragraph that tells all about that topic. Organize your information in a way that makes sense.	**2.** Suppose a new kid in class needs to find his or her way to the gym. Write a set of directions that tell how to get from your classroom to the gym. Be sure to write the directions in order from first to last.
A SOCIAL STUDIES REPORT	**A SCIENCE REPORT**
3. Use online information, the library, and adults you know to find the answer to this question: How did my town get its name? Learn as much as you can about the name of your town or city. Write what you learn in a report that answers the question.	**4.** Use Althea's plan to write a report on an unusual pet. Some ideas are below, but there are many others! Find information about the pet online or in the library. Take notes. Organize your notes. Think of a good way to share your finished report with the class. Add pictures that you draw or print from the Internet. caiman degu pot-bellied pig

W.3.3	Write narratives to develop real or imagined experiences or events using effective technique, descriptive details, and clear event sequences. **a.** Establish a situation and introduce a narrator and/or characters; organize an event sequence that unfolds naturally. **b.** Use dialogue and descriptions of actions, thoughts, and feelings to develop experiences and events or show the response of characters to situations. **c.** Use temporal words and phrases to signal event order. **d.** Provide a sense of closure.
CCR.W.3	Write narratives to develop real or imagined experiences or events using effective technique, well-chosen details, and well-structured event sequences.
CCR.W.6	Use technology, including the Internet, to produce and publish writing and to interact and collaborate with others.
L.3.3	Use knowledge of language and its conventions when writing, speaking, reading, or listening. **b.** Recognize and observe differences between the conventions of spoken and written standard English.

 ## Understand the Standards

A sitcom is a half-hour show on TV. A sitcom has a funny story line. The characters are made up, and so is the action. Someone writes the story for each week's show.

> **Words to Know**
> entertain
> narrative
> narrator
> personal narrative
> dialogue

All sitcoms are narratives. That just means they tell a story. They tell it through dialogue and action. Written stories may tell a story the same way. They use words to describe the action. Written stories often have a narrator who tells the story to the reader.

Writing Connection

When you write to **entertain,** you try to amuse or interest your reader.

- A **narrative** is a story. It has a beginning, middle, and end.

- A **narrator** is the person who tells a story.

- A **personal narrative** is a true story told by the person who lived it.

- **Dialogue** is the words that people speak in a narrative.

Narrative Prompt

Real World Connection

> The story writer Stephen King once said, "A place is yours when you know where all the roads go." Think back to when you started school. At what point did you know your way around? When did it stop feeling scary? At what point did the school become "yours"? Write a personal narrative for new students. Tell about the time when the school became "yours." Tell what you felt, said, and did.

Planning

Purpose and Audience

Before you write, think about why you are writing. Think about who will read your writing. This will help you prepare to write the best story you can write.

Use the prompt to answer these questions.

1. Why are you writing a personal narrative?

_____

2. Who will read your personal narrative?

_____

3. Who will be the narrator of your story?

_____

Prewriting

Writing a personal narrative is a lot like writing any story. You need to think about the characters. You need to think about the setting and the plot. You need to tell what happened in an order that makes sense.

Tia used a story organizer to write some ideas about her story.

Characters: me, Mom, Mrs. Streeter, Paul		Setting: our school
Beginning	Middle	End
starting kindergarten	take bus day 2	first day of week 2
big building	get lost	walk in right door
long hallways	Mrs. Streeter	go right to cubby
Mom drives me	finds me	show Paul where to go

Use Tia's notes to answer these questions.

1. How does Tia's story begin?

_____

2. How does Tia's story end?

_____

Drafting

Organizing

Tia's story organizer will help her write her story in order. Most stories are in time order. They start by introducing the main character, setting, and situation.

> The first day of kindergarten, Mom drove me to school.
>
> I walked into the big building. I walked down the long
>
> hallway. How would I ever find my classroom without
>
> Mom to help me?

Answer these questions about Tia's opening paragraph.

1. Which parts tell about the setting of the story? Circle them.

2. Which part tells the narrator's problem? Underline it.

3. Tia is writing for new students. How might the problem she introduces interest and entertain new students?

_____

_____

Time-Order Words

You can use special words to show the order of events. This box shows some examples.

first	second	then	after	before

Add time-order words to these sentences in Tia's story.

_____ I walked into the big building. _____ I walked down the long hallway.

Dialogue

Stories can use dialogue instead of description to tell what happens. Tia added a sentence of dialogue to her paragraph.

> The first day of kindergarten, Mom drove me to school. I walked into the big building. I walked down the long hallway. "I'm worried," I had told Mom. How would I ever find my classroom without Mom to help me?

What does the dialogue tell you about the narrator?

_____

Revising and Editing

Revising for Content and Argument

After you write, read your work. Have a classmate or an adult read it, too. Use this checklist to see what you might fix.

> REVISING NARRATIVE WRITING
> ❑ Can my reader tell what the setting of my story is?
> ❑ Are my sentences all about the same topic?
> ❑ Did I use dialogue and description to show how characters feel?

Read the middle of Tia's story. Look at the changes she made.

On day 2, I took the bus. Sure enough, I got

in the maze of hallways   "There you are, Tia!" she said kindly.
lost. Mrs. Streeter came looking for me. She took my
       ∧   ∧

hand and led me to class.

Answer these questions about Tia's edited paragraph.

1. How does the description of the hallways help you picture Tia's problem?

_____

2. What do you learn about Mrs. Streeter from the addition of dialogue?

_____

Revising for Clarity and Style

Revise your writing to make it clear and easy
to read.

Tia thought about the prompt. Then she added
something to her story ending.

REVISING NARRATIVE
WRITING
❏ Does my story have
a clear beginning,
middle, and end?
❏ Do my characters act
and speak in ways that
seem real?

I followed other kids for the rest of the week. Then, on Monday

of week 2, I marched off the bus and into the right door. I found

my cubby right away. I even showed Paul how to get to his
I felt safe and smart. School wasn't so big and scary after all!
classroom!
          ∧

How do Tia's sentences improve her ending?

Proofreading

Before you finish writing, look for mistakes using the checklist to the right.

Tia made some mistakes when she copied her story over. Use the proofreading marks in Appendix 2 to proofread this part of Tia's story.

> PROOFREADING CHECKLIST
> ❑ Did I indent my paragraphs?
> ❑ Did I use capital letters correctly?
> ❑ Did I use punctuation marks correctly?
> ❑ Did I spell all words correctly?

> On day 2, I took the bus. Sure enough, I got lost in the maze of halways. Mrs Streeter came looking for me. "There you are, tia! she said kindly. She took my hand and led me to class.

Publishing

Your story is not finished until you share it with your audience.

Sitcom writers publish their work on TV. Tia decided to act out her story with some friends.

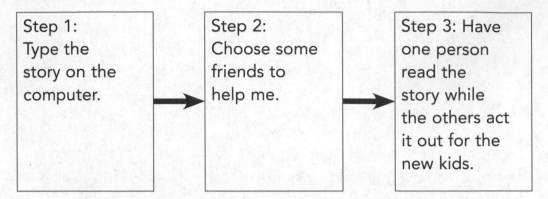

| Step 1: Type the story on the computer. | Step 2: Choose some friends to help me. | Step 3: Have one person read the story while the others act it out for the new kids. |

Work with some friends. Read and act out Tia's story.

> Learning My School
> by Tia R.
>
> The first day of kindergarten, Mom drove me to school. First, I walked into the big building. Then, I walked down the long hallway. "I'm worried," I had told Mom. How would I ever find my classroom without Mom to help me?
>
> On day 2, I took the bus. Sure enough, I got lost in the maze of hallways. Mrs. Streeter came looking for me. "There you are, Tia!" she said kindly. She took my hand and led me to class.
>
> I followed other kids for the rest of the week. Then, on Monday of week 2, I marched off the bus and into the right door. I found my cubby right away. I even showed Paul how to get to his classroom! I felt safe and smart. The school wasn't so big and scary after all!

On Your Own

Choose one of these prompts. Follow the steps in this lesson to do your own narrative writing.

A SITCOM	A FAIRY TALE
1. Write a funny scene of dialogue that could be part of a sitcom. Tell what happens between two friends in a lunchroom. One child wants to trade sandwiches with the other. The second child is not sure he or she wants to trade.	**2.** Imagine that a child finds a magic shoe lying on the sidewalk. What happens next? Write a story to entertain young children. Tell the story of the magic shoe. Use dialogue and description. Give your story a clear beginning, middle, and end.
A SHORT STORY	**A PERSONAL NARRATIVE**
3. Use this story organizer to write a short story. Use time-order words to tell what happens first, next, and last. <u>Characters</u>: boy, dog <u>Setting</u>: swamp <u>Beginning</u>: A boy and his dog go for a walk. <u>Middle</u>: They find something surprising. <u>End</u>: They decide what to do about it.	**4.** Think about a time when you felt lonely. Why did you feel that way? What did you do to help yourself? Write a personal narrative that tells about that time. Make sure that your reader can tell how you felt, what you said, and what you did. Give your story an ending that tells how you solved your problem.

Write an Article about a National Holiday

Every country in the world celebrates certain days of the year. We celebrate days that are important to our history or our culture. Here are some of the national holidays we celebrate in the United States:

- Fourth of July
- Labor Day
- Martin Luther King Jr. Day
- Thanksgiving

Form a small group with a few classmates. Each person chooses a national holiday. Use the list above, or find another national holiday you like to celebrate. Write a short article telling people about your chosen holiday. Here are questions you should answer in your article:

- When does this holiday take place every year? When was it created?
- What do we celebrate on this day?
- Why is it important to celebrate these people or events?

Edit your articles carefully to correct any mistakes in grammar or spelling. Write the final drafts out neatly by hand, or type them up. Display them on a bulletin board in the classroom, along with pictures of holiday celebrations.

Start a Story from a Sentence

Form a group with six to eight of your classmates. Each person writes the first sentence of a short story on a slip of paper. It can be about anything you like.

Collect all the slips of paper, fold them so the writing doesn't show, and put them in a box. Mix up the folded papers and have each student draw one. If you draw your own sentence, set it aside, draw another slip, and then return your sentence to the box.

Using the opening sentence you chose, write a complete short story. It should be from one to five pages long, and you can add illustrations if you like. Take a day or two for writing and polishing stories before the group meets again. Share and discuss the stories you wrote.

Publish a Newspaper

Work with a small group of classmates. Together, you will write the first issue of a class newspaper.

Each person should write one article for the newspaper. Newspapers can include many different kinds of stories. Here are some ideas to get you started:

- a recipe for a favorite snack or dessert

- an account of a recent field trip, or a preview of one that is coming up soon

- an interview with a teacher

- a short story or poem

- a review of a student play or concert

Take a day or two to write, edit, and polish your articles. Once all the articles are finished, use the computer to lay them out in newspaper format. Print enough copies of the newspaper for the entire class.

Create a Pair of Informational Essays

Choose a partner. Together, find a pair of two different insects or animals that are hard for most people to tell apart. Here are some suggestions to get you started:

- butterfly and moth
- frog and toad
- alligator and crocodile
- bee and wasp

You take one animal of the pair, and your partner takes the other. On your own, find out facts about your animal. Look for information about where it lives, what it eats, how big it is, what colors it comes in, and things like that. Use what you learn to write a paragraph describing your animal.

Get together with your partner and read each other's paragraphs. Use your information to collaborate on an essay that tells how your animals/insects are alike and how they are different. Edit and proofread your essay. Add pictures of the animals or insects you wrote about.

CCR.L.1/L.3.1: Demonstrate command of the conventions of standard English grammar and usage when writing or speaking.

CCR.L.2/L.3.2: Demonstrate command of the conventions of standard English capitalization, punctuation, and spelling when writing.

Mini-Lesson 1   Common and Proper Nouns

L.3.1.a   Explain the function of nouns, pronouns, verbs, adjectives, and adverbs in general and their functions in particular sentences.

- A **noun** usually names a person, a place, or a thing.

- A **common noun** names any person, place, or thing.

  Examples: parent, dentist, friend / city, lake, school / shoe, computer, sandwich

- A **proper noun** names a specific person, place, or thing.

  Examples: Mom, Dr. Lin, Chris / Houston, Lake Erie, Grant Elementary School / Rockrunner, Alpha-100, Big Burger Blast

 On Your Own

Read each noun. Write whether it names a person, a place, or a thing. Then write whether it is common or proper.

1 neighbor _____ _____

2 Park Avenue _____ _____

3 Uncle David _____ _____

4 bicycle _____ _____

5 Mrs. Johnson _____ _____

6 classroom _____ _____

7 Grand Canyon _____ _____

8 Thunder Drum Company _____ _____

Mini-Lesson 2 Abstract Nouns

L.3.1.c   Use abstract nouns.

An **abstract noun** names an idea.

Examples: life, freedom, sadness, hope, friendship, power

 On Your Own

Circle the abstract noun in each group of words.

1	airplane	anger	author
2	carpet	cereal	courage
3	keyboard	kindness	knight
4	skill	snowflake	stripe
5	valley	vegetable	victory

Mini-Lesson 3 Singular and Plural Nouns

L.3.1.b   Form and use regular and irregular plural nouns.

- A **singular noun** names one person, place, thing, or idea.

- A **plural noun** names more than one person, place, thing, or idea.

- To turn many singular nouns into plural nouns, add -s to the singular noun. Some singular nouns form their plural in other ways.

Examples:

Singular	Plural
book, house, key	books, houses, keys
glass, peach, fox	glasses, peaches, foxes
baby, party, cherry	babies, parties, cherries
leaf, knife, thief	leaves, knives, thieves

deer, sheep, scissors   deer, sheep, scissors

tooth, woman, child   teeth, women, children

 On Your Own

Complete each sentence. Write the plural form of each noun in parentheses ( ).

1 The _____ around here have big _____.
    (beach)   (wave)

2 Did your _____ get caught in those _____?
    (foot)   (bush)

3 Both of my _____ have had exciting _____.
    (grandfather)   (life)

4 Aunt Mae's _____ are as quiet as _____.
    (kiss)   (butterfly)

5 Two _____ are eating the _____ in our garden!
    (moose)   (berry)

Mini-Lesson 4   Pronouns

L.3.1.a   Explain the function of nouns, pronouns, verbs, adjectives, and adverbs in general and their functions in particular sentences.

○ A **pronoun** is a word that can take the place of a noun or nouns.

Examples: I, you, he, she, it, we, you, they, me, you, him, her, it, us, you, them, my/mine, your/yours, his, her/hers, its, our/ours, your/yours, their/theirs

○ The pronoun that you use depends on its job in the sentence.

Example: Anita writes good **songs. She** sings **them** at school.

On Your Own

Read each sentence. Write the pronoun that can take the place of the word or words in parentheses ( ).

1 (Peter) is the best player on the soccer team. _____

2 Hey, Emily, Mrs. Ryan is looking for (Emily)! _____

3 Tonight (Tomás and Beth) will go to the library. _____

4 Everyone in class held (the tiny chick). _____

5 Olivia could not find (Olivia's) blue jacket. _____

6 May (Steve and I) watch a movie? _____

7 Roberto says that this book is (Roberto's). _____

8 Our parents gave (the new teachers) a party. _____

Mini-Lesson 5   Pronoun-Antecedent Agreement

L.3.1.f   Ensure subject-verb and pronoun-antecedent agreement.

- An **antecedent** is the word or words that a pronoun replaces.

- Every pronoun must **agree** with, or match, its antecedent.

Examples: Justin is reading its report. (INCORRECT)

Justin is reading **his** report. (CORRECT)

I watched the **birds** and fed it, too. (INCORRECT)

I watched the **birds** and fed **them,** too. (CORRECT)

On Your Own

Circle each correct pronoun choice.

1   Mrs. Jacobs is my teacher, and (she, her) knows a lot!

2   You and I had the best science project. The prize belongs to (us, me).

3   Class, here are some homework questions. (You, They) should not be too difficult.

4   I saw a large shape swim by. (It, I) was a whale!

5   Marcus loves all kinds of stories, but mysteries are (their, his) favorite kind.

Mini-Lesson 6   Kinds of Verbs

L.3.1.a   Explain the function of nouns, pronouns, verbs, adjectives, and adverbs in general and their functions in particular sentences.

○ An **action verb** is a word that shows what someone or something does, thinks, or says.

Example: The soccer players **raced** down the field.

○ A **linking verb** is a word that shows what someone or something is. Many linking verbs are forms of the verb *be.*

Example: Grandma and Grandpa **are** very cheerful people.

○ The **main verb** in a sentence can be action or linking. Sometimes a **helping verb** works with the main verb.

Example: Everyone **has** worked hard on the play. It **will** be the best one yet!

 On Your Own

Look at the underlined verb in each sentence. Write *A* if it is an action verb. Write *L* if it is a linking verb. Write *H* if it is a helping verb.

1   I <u>was</u> happy about my friend's good news. _____

2   Lauren <u>will</u> read twenty books this summer. _____

3 Every weekend, Zach <u>runs</u> two miles. _____

4 Julia and her parents <u>have</u> gone to the state fair. _____

5 My brother Paul <u>is</u> a great trumpet player. _____

6 Tina's cat <u>watched</u> the birds outside all day. _____

7 You <u>should</u> follow this map carefully. _____

8 My neighbors <u>grow</u> vegetables in their garden. _____

Mini-Lesson 7   Verb Tenses

L.3.1.e   Form and use the simple verb tenses..

- **Tense** is the time that a verb shows.

- A verb in the **past tense** shows what happened or was in the past.

  Example: My family and I **visited** the zoo last week.

- A verb in the **present tense** shows what happens or is now.

  Example: In fact, we **visit** the zoo often.

- A verb in the **future tense** shows what will happen or will be.

  Example: We probably **will visit** again soon.

 On Your Own

Look at the underlined verb in each sentence. Write whether it is in the past tense, the present tense, or the future tense.

1 Our dogs <u>bark</u> at almost anything! _____

2 Tomorrow my team <u>will play</u> an important game. _____

3 Last night, Mom's flight <u>arrived</u> an hour late. _____

4 Those <u>were</u> the funniest movies ever! _____

5 My friends and I <u>study</u> together after class. _____

6 Field Day <u>will be</u> a great time for our class. _____

7 Maria just <u>saw</u> a hummingbird in her garden. _____

8 <u>Will</u> you <u>come</u> to Noah's birthday party? _____

Mini-Lesson 8   Regular and Irregular Verbs

L.3.1.d   Form and use regular and irregular verbs.

- Verbs have different forms to show different tenses.

- For the present tense, use most verbs as they are. Sometimes add *-s* or *-es*.

    Examples: We **paint** great pictures in art class. Mr. Lee **teaches** us well.

- For the future tense, write *will* before the verb.

    Example: I **will walk** to the park after lunch.

- For the past tense of some verbs, add *-ed* to the verb.

    Example: With a smile, Jim **opened** the box.

- Many verbs form their past tense in other ways.

    Examples:

<u>Verb</u>	<u>Past Tense</u>
bake, live	baked, lived
cry, hurry	cried, hurried
grab, stop	grabbed, stopped
come, get	came, got
bring, think	brought, thought
be	was/were

       Measuring Up® to the Common Core

On Your Own

Read each sentence. Circle the correct past-tense verb form.

1 Chase and I (studyed, studied) at his house.

2 At lunchtime, Danielle and Ben (traded, tradeed) sandwiches.

3 Last night, I (wished, wosh) upon a star.

4 My cousin (drived, drove) us to the swimming pool.

5 We (missed, mist) the school bus this morning.

6 Late in the day, the skies (becomed, became) cloudy.

7 The rabbit (hopped, hoped) into the garden.

8 At the last minute, Isabel (caught, catched) the ball!

Mini-Lesson 9   Subject-Verb Agreement

L.3.1.f   Ensure subject-verb and pronoun-antecedent agreement.

- A **subject** is the person, place, or thing that a sentence is about. A subject *does* something (action verb) or *is* something (linking verb).

- Every verb must agree with, or match, its subject.

Examples: Those **movies** was too scary for me. (INCORRECT)

Those **movies were** too scary for me. (CORRECT)

This **book** about whales have great pictures. (INCORRECT)

This **book** about whales **has** great pictures. (CORRECT)

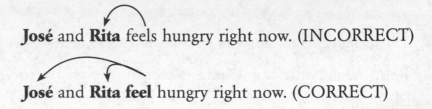

José and **Rita** feels hungry right now. (INCORRECT)

José and **Rita** feel hungry right now. (CORRECT)

 On Your Own

Circle each correct verb choice.

1 The boxes in the garage (is, are) very heavy.

2 Every evening, Dr. Jones (takes, take) a long walk.

3 Radio and TV (gives, give) us the daily news.

4 The writer of these stories often (surprises, surprise) us.

5 That big octopus (looks, look) mean to Sue and me.

6 My teammates and our coach (is, are) ready for the game.

7 Activities after school (includes, include) Choir and Science Club.

8 My dog Comet and I (are, am) the best of friends.

Mini-Lesson 10   Adjectives

L.3.1.a   Explain the function of nouns, pronouns, verbs, adjectives, and adverbs in general and their functions in particular sentences.

○ An **adjective** is a describing word. It shows what a person, place, or thing is like. It can answer a question such as *What kind? Which one?* or *How many?*

Examples: green leaves   **sunny** beach   **wonderful** doctor

three new books   a **large** but **friendly** dog

On Your Own

Look at the underlined noun in each sentence. Circle each adjective that describes that noun. (Some nouns have one adjective. A few have two adjectives.)

1 Rachel sped down the street on her red <u>bicycle</u>.

2 Last night I wrote a long <u>letter</u> to Grandpa Jack.

3 The gravel made a loud and crunchy <u>sound</u> under my feet.

4 There must have been forty <u>people</u> on line ahead of us!

5 Linda smiled as she held the small, fluffy <u>duckling</u>.

Mini-Lesson 11   Comparing with Adjectives

L.3.1.g   Form and use comparative and superlative adjectives and adverbs, and choose between them depending on what is to be modified.

- Some adjectives compare people, places, or things.

- A **comparative adjective** compares two people, places, or things. Add -*er* to most short adjectives to make them comparative. Write *more* before long adjectives to make them comparative.

  Examples: sharp—sharp**er**   beautiful—**more** beautiful

- A **superlative adjective** compares three or more people, places, or things. Add -*est* to most short adjectives to make them superlative. Write *most* before long adjectives to make them superlative.

  Examples: sharp—sharp**est**   beautiful—**most** beautiful

On Your Own

Circle each correct adjective choice. Write *C* if it is a comparative adjective. Write *S* if it is a superlative adjective.

1 Friday was a (warmer, warmest) day than today. _____

2 Of us three brothers, Jeremy is the (taller, tallest) one. _____

3 Shayla is the (more creative, most creative) person I know. _____

4 The mountains have the (most peaceful, peacefulest) scenery

in the country. _____

5 I want to watch TV, but this math homework is a (valuabler, more valuable)

way to spend my time. _____

Mini-Lesson 12   Adverbs

L.3.1.a   Explain the function of nouns, pronouns, verbs, adjectives, and adverbs in general and their functions in particular sentences.

○ An **adverb** is a describing word. It shows more about the action of a verb. It can answer a question such as *How? When?* or *Where?*

Examples: The skies **suddenly** opened.   Rain fell **hard.**

Darrell and his sister **quickly** ran **inside.**

 On Your Own

Look at the underlined verb in each sentence. Circle each adverb that describes that verb. (Some verbs have one adverb. A few have two adverbs.)

1 Kris <u>spoke</u> softly to the crying child.

2 I never <u>remember</u> the answer to that riddle!

3 Allison said goodbye and then <u>walked</u> away.

4 Coach Jackson <u>will have</u> water for the players nearby.

5 Yesterday Elena <u>sang</u> well in the voice contest.

Mini-Lesson 13   Comparing with Adverbs

L.3.1.g Form and use comparative and superlative adjectives and adverbs, and choose between them depending on what is to be modified.

○ Some adverbs compare the actions of verbs.

○ A **comparative adverb** compares two actions. Add *-er* to most short adverbs to make them comparative. Write *more* before adverbs that end in *-ly* to make them comparative.

    Examples: soon–soon**er**   quietly–**more** quietly

○ A **superlative adverb** compares three or more actions. Add *-est* to most short adverbs to make them superlative. Write *most* before adverbs that end in *-ly* to make them superlative.

    Examples: soon–soon**est**   quietly–**most** quietly

 On Your Own

Complete each sentence with the correct form of the adverb in parentheses ( ). Write *C* if it is a comparative adverb. Write *S* if it is a superlative adverb.

1 Sam worked _____ on the project than I did. _____
      (hard)

2 Of the four kittens, the gray one meows _____. _____
                (noisily)

3 No one speaks _____ than Aunt Beth does. _____
      (wisely)

4 Greg practices guitar several times a day. He practices _____,
(long)

however, after supper. _____

5 After I fell, I walked along _____ . _____
(carefully)

Mini-Lesson 14   Adjective or Adverb?

L.3.1.g   Form and use comparative and superlative adjectives and adverbs, and choose between them depending on what is to be modified.

° When you use describing words, think carefully. Be sure to use an adjective to describe a noun. Be sure to use an adverb to describe a verb.

Example: The dancers moved **graceful** onto the stage. (INCORRECT)

The dancers moved **gracefully** onto the stage. (CORRECT)

° A few words can be adjectives in some sentences and adverbs in others.

Example: We arrived **late** for the **late** show!
(adverb)   (adjective)

 On Your Own

Look at the underlined word in each sentence. Write whether it is an adjective or an adverb. If it is used correctly, write *correct*. If it is incorrect, write the correct form.

1 Mom always says, "The <u>early</u> bird catches the worm."

_____ _____

2 Nathan turned red and grinned <u>bashful</u> at us.

_____ _____

3 The boat sank <u>lower</u> in the water.

_____ _____

4 The <u>nervously</u> worker dropped a stack of dishes.

_____ _____

5 After a scolding, little Anisha acted <u>politer</u>.

_____ _____

Mini-Lesson 15   Conjunctions

L.3.1.h   Use coordinating and subordinating conjunctions.

- A **conjunction** is a connecting word. It can connect words or groups of words.

- A **coordinating conjunction** connects things that are equal. Coordinating conjunctions include *and*, *but*, and *or*.

  Examples: My favorite colors are <u>red</u> **and** <u>blue</u>.

  <u>We had a flat tire</u>, **but** <u>Mom fixed it</u>.

  The box is <u>on the table</u> **or** <u>in the garage</u>.

- A **subordinating conjunction** connects ideas that are not equal. The subordinating conjunction begins the less important idea. Subordinating conjunctions include *as*, *because*, *if*, and *when*.

  Examples: **As** <u>Matt watched</u>, <u>the balloons rose into the sky</u>.

  <u>Maria felt sad</u> **because** <u>her friend moved away</u>.

  <u>I will help you</u> **if** <u>you wish</u>.

  When <u>we make pizza</u>, <u>we always have a good time</u>.

On Your Own

Read each sentence. Circle the conjunction that makes better sense. Write *C* if it is a coordinating conjunction. Write *S* if it is a subordinating conjunction.

1 We will take salad (but, or) rolls to the picnic. _____

2 Brian shouted (and, because) he was far away from us. _____

3 That store is open late on Friday (and, if) again on Saturday. _____

4 Elena will write a letter (but, when) she has time. _____

5 (As, If) I guessed, we had a spelling test today. _____

Mini-Lesson 16   Three Kinds of Sentences

L.3.1.i   Produce simple, compound, and complex sentences.

- **Sentences** are groups of words that express complete thoughts.

- A **simple sentence** expresses one complete thought.

   Example: Ethan drew a funny picture of his dog.

- A **compound sentence** expresses two or more complete but equal thoughts.

   Example: The phone rang ten times, but no one answered.

- A **complex sentence** expresses two or more complete thoughts, but at least one thought is less important.

   Example: You were born in Miami, as **I recall.**

On Your Own

Read each sentence. Underline each complete thought. Then write whether the sentence is simple, compound, or complex.

1 This book is long, but it tells a great story. _____

2 I sometimes see deer at the edge of the woods. _____

3 We moved to Boston because Dad got a job there. _____

4 The vase on the table held a dozen white roses. _____

5 If the test is tomorrow, Grace will be ready. _____

6 Kevin had a great idea, and we listened carefully. _____

7 When Mom called Adam and me, we came right away. _____

8 Do you want a snack, or can you wait for supper? _____

Mini-Lesson 17   Capital Letters in Titles

L.3.2.a   Capitalize appropriate words in titles.

○ A **title** is the name of a book, movie, poem, song, and so on.

○ Capitalize the first word and the last word in a title.

○ Capitalize every noun, pronoun, verb, adjective, and adverb.

○ Do not capitalize these words unless they appear first in a title.

     a,   an,   the,   and,   but,   or,   to

Examples: *It Was an Early Morning* (book)

          Morgan and the Mysterious Message (movie)

          "We Quietly Watched the Starry Sky" (poem)

          "When Love Is Not a Dream" (song)

On Your Own

Read each title. Circle each word that should be capitalized.

1 *find a silver mountain*

2 "an odd otter or an eager eagle"

3 *ron rumpus and the rickety red robot*

4 "but sometimes we still wonder"

5 "beyond the clouds or moon or sun"

Mini-Lesson 18   Commas in Addresses

L.3.2.b   Use commas in addresses.

- Put **commas** after a city and state or city and country in a sentence.

   Example: My cousin from Lima, Peru, sent me a letter.

- Sometimes you may write a complete address in a sentence. Put a comma after the street and after the city. Do not put a comma after the state if you write the ZIP code.

   Example: Mr. Moore delivered the package to 1470 Harbor Road, Oakland, California 94619.

 On Your Own

Add commas to these sentences where needed.

1 My uncle from Toledo Ohio is coming to visit.

2 Did you mean Paris France or Paris Texas?

3 Hakim and Farrah live at 63 Elm Street Portland.

4 My aunt's new address is 155 North 40th Street Tampa Florida 33610.

5 That business has moved to 469 Fifth Avenue New York New York 10010.

Mini-Lesson 19 — Commas and Quotation Marks in Dialogue

L.3.2.c   Use commas and quotation marks in dialogue.

- Use **quotation marks** to show the words that someone says. These words are called a **quotation**. People say words to each other in a **dialogue**.

- Sometimes a quotation begins a sentence. Write a comma before you write the last quotation marks. Then name the speaker.

    Example: "This is a good book," **Riley said.**

- Sometimes a quotation ends a sentence. Write a comma after you name the speaker. Then write the last quotation marks after the period.

Example: She told Mike, "You just might enjoy it."

 On Your Own

Add quotation marks and commas to this dialogue where needed.

1 Mike said I have heard of this writer.

2 She has won many awards he added.

3 Riley answered She may win another one for this book.

4 It is the best mystery story ever she told him.

5 Mike, you may borrow it when I finish she promised.

Mini-Lesson 20   Possessives

L.3.2.d   Form and use possessives.

- A **possessive** is a word that shows that someone owns something.

- To form the possessive of a singular noun, add -'s.

   Examples: a dog's bark   Dad's job   Carmen's house

- To form the possessive of many plural nouns, add just -'.

   Examples: the cooks' hats   the lions' roars

- To form the possessive of plural nouns that don't already end in -s, add -'s.

   Examples: two women's gifts   all the children's books

- Possessive pronouns have their own special forms.

   Examples: my/mine, your/yours, his, her/hers, its,
   our/ours, your/yours, their/theirs

 On Your Own

Circle each correct possessive.

1   Hey, I just found (Daniels', Daniel's) jacket!

2   Mikayla writes poems, and this is one of (hers, her's).

3   Those three (teacher's, teachers') classes are fun.

4   The (men's, mens') suits look expensive.

5   I have my book, so this book must be (their's, theirs).

6   Those (baby's, babies') pictures are really cute.

7   (Dr. Lewis's, Dr. Lewis') son is in the U.S. Army.

8   One (deers', deer's) fawn kept close to (its, it's) mother.

Mini-Lesson 21   Spelling

L.3.2.e   Use conventional spelling for high-frequency and other studied words and for adding suffixes to base words.

L.3.2.f   Use spelling patterns and generalizations in writing words.

L.3.2.g   Consult reference materials, including beginning dictionaries, as needed to check and correct spellings.

○ Knowing how to spell correctly is important. Here are 75 words that third-graders should be able to spell.

about	impossible	state
again	independent	terrible
always	knew	their
another	know	there
are	little	thought
beautiful	lovable	threw
because	moaning	through
brain	neighbor	title
caught	new	to
coast	nickel	too
could	one	trained
countries	our	treat
discovery	outdoors	two
distant	overcome	unhappiness
eighty	pattern	uniform
enough	peaceful	unknown
everyone	probably	usable
except	purple	usual
favorite	puzzle	vacant
flight	question	wear
governor	right	weather
hammer	robber	where
hidden	said	winner
home	semicircle	won
hopeful	something	write

On Your Own

Look at the underlined words in each sentence. Circle the word that is spelled incorrectly. Then write the correct spelling on the line. If you need to, use a dictionary.

1 When Katy <u>through</u> the ball, Evan <u>caught</u> it. _____.

2 The <u>vacent</u> house had a <u>hidden</u> secret. _____.

3 Is this <u>purple</u> coat <u>useable</u>? _____.

4 "That is <u>impossable</u>," Mrs. Wilson <u>said</u>. _____.

5 Amber <u>thought</u> that the <u>puzzle</u> was <u>to</u> hard. _____.

6 The <u>weather</u> along the <u>coast</u> is <u>beutiful</u>. _____.

7 Jon's <u>favorite</u> band just <u>one</u> <u>another</u> award. _____.

8 <u>Out doors</u> is <u>where</u> we <u>always</u> like <u>to</u> play. _____.

SL.3.1	Engage effectively in a range of collaborative discussions with diverse partners on *grade 3 topics and texts*, building on others' ideas and expressing their own clearly.
	a. Come to discussions prepared, having read or studied required material; explicitly draw on that preparation and other information known about the topic to explore ideas under discussion.
	b. Follow agreed-upon rules for discussions.
	c. Ask questions to check understanding of information presented, stay on topic, and link their comments to the remarks of others.
	d. Explain their own ideas and understanding in light of the discussion.
SL.3.2	Determine the main ideas and supporting details of a text read aloud or information presented in diverse media and formats, including visually, quantitatively, and orally.
SL.3.3	Ask and answer questions about information from a speaker, offering appropriate elaboration and detail.
SL.3.4	Report on a topic or text, tell a story, or recount an experience with appropriate facts and relevant, descriptive details, speaking clearly at an understandable pace.
SL.3.5	Create engaging audio recordings of stories or poems that demonstrate fluid reading at an understandable pace; add visual displays when appropriate to emphasize or enhance certain facts or details.
SL.3.6	Speak in complete sentences when appropriate to task and situation in order to provide requested detail or clarification.
CCR.SL.2	Integrate and evaluate information presented in diverse media and formats, including visually, quantitatively, and orally.
CCR.SL.5	Make strategic use of digital media and visual displays of data to exapress information and enhance understanding of presentations.

Mini-Lesson 1 — Listening to an Informative Explanatory Presentation

SL.3.1.a Come to discussions prepared, having read or studied required material; explicitly draw on that preparation and other information known about the topic to explore ideas under discussion.

Introduction

Imagine yourself on a field trip to the zoo. You learn about strange and unfamiliar animals. Some of what you learn comes from studying the animals close up and telling others what you see. Some of what you learn is what animal experts at the zoo tell you in a talk. The speaker gives facts and explains how the facts are connected.

Make It Work

When you listen in class, when you go on field trips, always be an active listener. Think about what you already know about the topic. Read what you were supposed to read. Compare what the speaker tells you with what you know on your own. Think of questions to ask.

Put It Together

Make a personal checklist for being an active listener. Make at least three entries. Add more during the year.

Active Listening Checklist

_____

_____

_____

_____

Mini-Lesson 2 — Listening to Texts and Presentations

SL.3.2   Determine the main ideas and supporting details of a text read aloud or information presented in diverse media and formats, including visually, quantitatively, and orally.

SL.3.3   Ask and answer questions about information from a speaker, offering appropriate elaboration and detail.

CCR.SL.2   Integrate and evaluate information presented in diverse media and formats, including visually, quantitatively, and orally.

 Introduction

Sometimes your teacher may read a book aloud to your class. You may be told to watch a video on the internet or watch a science experiment being done. How can you get the most from these experiences?

 Make It Work

Listen for main ideas and details. Remember that the main idea does not have to be the first thing the speaker reads or says. The main idea helps you understand how the other ideas are connected.

Listen actively by taking notes. Organize the information you hear by using a diagram like this one:

Main Idea:		
Detail:	Detail:	Detail:

Put It Together

Listen carefully as your teacher reads a passage from a book aloud. Come prepared to listen actively by making an organizer like the one above. Afterwards, compare your notes with your classmates' notes. Create a final set of notes about the passage.

Mini-Lesson 3   Speaking in a Group Setting

SL.3.1.b	Follow agreed-upon rules for discussions.
SL.3.1.c	Ask questions to check understanding of information presented, stay on topic, and link their comments to the remarks of others.
SL.3.1.d	Explain their own ideas and understanding in light of the discussion.
SL.3.6	Speak in complete sentences when appropriate to task and situation in order to provide requested detail or clarification.

 Introduction

Is this familiar? You're with a bunch of people and everyone is talking at the same time. Only the loudest person gets heard. That may be fine on the weekend, with friends. It doesn't work too well in school, though, where your purpose is to learn.

 Make It Work

Here are some useful rules to follow. They will make discussions run smoothly.

Checklist for Speaking

☐ Look at your audience.

☐ Speak loudly enough that others can understand you.

☐ Speak slowly enough that you don't sound rushed.

☐ Speak in full sentences.

☐ Speak with expression.

☐ Stay on topic.

☐ Explain your ideas and answer questions.

Put It Together

Discuss the checklist with a small group of classmates. Decide what "loudly enough," "slowly enough," and "with expression" mean. On your own, practice reading a short passage aloud so that it follows the guidelines well.

Mini-Lesson 4   Making Presentations

SL.3.4	Report on a topic or text, tell a story, or recount an experience with appropriate facts and relevant, descriptive details, speaking clearly at an understandable pace.
SL.3.5	Create engaging audio recordings of stories or poems that demonstrate fluid reading at an understandable pace; add visual displays when appropriate to emphasize or enhance certain facts or details.
CCR.SL.2	Integrate and evaluate information presented in diverse media and formats, including visually, quantitatively, and orally.
CCR.SL.5	Make strategic use of digital media and visual displays of data to express information and enhance understanding of presentations.

 Introduction

Have you listened to a speaker who mumbles or who speaks so quickly or slowly that people stop listening? Or a speaker who doesn't have much to share? Don't let that speaker be you! Here are some ideas for making presentations that grab and hold people's attention.

 Make It Work

Have something interesting to say. Have an interesting or appealing way to present it.

If you are giving information or telling a story, do this:

- Stay on purpose.
- Do not stray from the topic.
- Give all important facts about the topic.
- Add details that help you give the full picture.
- Speak clearly and at a pace that will help your listeners understand you.

     Measuring Up® to the Common Core

Put It Together

Pick a favorite poem or passage that can stand alone. Then make an audio recording or a video of the poem or passage. Practice first so that your reading is fluid and expresses the full meaning of the text. Look around for photographs or other visual aids that you can show your audience to make the meaning of the text clearer.

Then create the audio or video recording of the text. Listen to it critically. Be sure that your reading is the best it can be. Leave time to do it over if you have to. Then present it to the class. Invite their comments and respond to them.

Mini-Lesson 5   Participating in Discussions

SL.3.1.b   Follow agreed-upon rules for discussions (e.g., gaining the floor in respectful ways, listening to others with care, speaking one at a time about the topics and texts under discussion).

SL.3.1.c   Ask questions to check understanding of information presented, stay on topic, and link their comments to the remarks of others.

 ## Introduction

Small-group discussions and large-group discussions happen all the time in school. Discussions are the most common way to put effective listening and speaking skills into practice.

It's a good idea every year to "discuss how to discuss." If you agree on rules for discussions, you will help your class discussions run smoothly for the rest of the year.

 ## Make It Work

Here are some rules that make discussions run smoothly. How would you change them to fit the needs of your class? What other rules would you add? Decide the answers to these questions in a small group. Then as a large group, reach an agreement about which rules work best for your class. Be sure that all ideas and suggestions stay on topic and build on what other students have said.

Here are some rules to start off with:

- Listen when others are speaking.
- Wait your turn to speak.
- Raise your hand to show you want the floor.
- Speak and listen with respect. Do not make faces or add side comments.
- Keep to the point.
- Use appropriate language.
- Encourage everyone to participate.

 Put It Together

Practice the rules that you agree on. Invite someone to be an observer during your discussions. Allow that person to point out when speakers and listeners have strayed from the agreed-on rules. Be committed to improving your discussion skills.

Organizer 1: Giving Reasons for an Opinion

Opinion:

Reason 1:

Reason 2:

Reason 3:

Organizer 2: Supporting an Opinion

Is _____ a good idea/plan/choice?

☐ YES   ☐ NO

Here's why I think so:

Reason 1: _____
_____
_____

Reason 2: _____
_____
_____

Reason 3: _____
_____
_____

Organizer 3: Grouping Ideas

My Notes About _____

Circle one group of notes that go together.

Underline a second group of notes that go together.

Box a third group of notes that go together.

Organizer 4: Outline for a Written or Oral Report

Title: _____

Paragraph I: Introduction

Paragraph II: _____

_____

_____

Paragraph III: _____

_____

_____

Paragraph IV: _____

_____

_____

Paragraph V: Conclusion

Organizer 5: Creating a Narrative

Characters:	Setting:

Beginning	Middle	End

Organizer 6: Telling a Story

PICTURE of the main character and the setting:

What happens FIRST:

What happens NEXT:

What happens LAST:

Appendix 2 Proofreading Marks

Proofreading Mark	Meaning	Example
≡	capitalize	we turned left onto ≡ beale street. ≡ ≡
⊙ or ∧̇	add a period	Please call Dr⊙ Jones tomorrow⊙
∧	add something	How much dos^e that ∧ pen cost ? ∧
∧	add a comma	Dinah∧did you call Minnie, Jake∧and Mo?
⌄⁹	add quotation marks	She asked, ⌄Did you buy any snacks?⌄
⌄	add an apostrophe	Don⌄t you think Mark⌄s story is good?
ℓ	take something away	Our class visited Washington℮, DC.

¶	indent the paragraph	¶Once upon a time, a toad lived under a stone wall. Living nearby were a chipmunk and a garter snake.
‿∧	respell or rewrite	Two wrongs do not right make a ~~write~~.∧
/	make a lowercase letter	Please ask your /Aunt to send me her /Recipe.
(move symbol)	move the text	I looked for my book around the room.

Writing Model 1: Opinion (Argument) Writing

The paragraph begins with a clear topic sentence that states the writer's opinion.

I believe that Louis Sachar is the best children's book writer of all. His Wayside School series has been my favorite since I started to read. His books are so funny! I can read them over and over and never get tired. The characters are crazy, but they seem like old friends. Since he writes for both girls and boys, anyone my age should try a book by Louis Sachar. He is a wonderful writer, and you will not be disappointed.

Reasons that support the opinion ("his books are so funny," "I can read them . . . and never get tired," "the characters . . . seem like old friends") appear in a logical order.

The writer uses linking words to connect opinions ("anyone my age should try a book by Louis Sachar") to reasons ("he writes for both girls and boys").

The paragraph ends with a concluding statement.

Writing Model 2: Informative/Explanatory Writing

Did you ever nap in a hammock? Hammocks have been around for a long time. They have been used for many reasons.

> The writer begins by introducing the topic.

A hammock is a bed made of cloth or string. It hangs by each end. It can swing back and forth.

> The writer may use definitions to develop the topic.

Hammocks were first used by Native Americans in Central and South America. They did not want snakes and bugs to bite them in the night. They hung their beds from trees.

Columbus brought hammocks home to Europe. In the 1500s, ships began to use them. Sailors could sleep well in hammocks. The hammocks were easy to move and put away.

> Facts and details appear in an order that makes sense. This writer used time order.

Today, soldiers may use hammocks. Astronauts may also use them. Of course, people use them in their yards. They make a nice place to rest and read.

> Linking words connect ideas that go together (soldiers use hammocks; astronauts also use hammocks).

> The writer includes a concluding section. Here, the writer tells how hammocks are still used today.

 Measuring Up® to the Common Core

Writing Model 3: Narrative Writing

At school, Mrs. Juno asked us how we got our names. I did not know why my name is Clara Louise. I decided to ask my mom.

> The story beginning introduces the characters, setting, and situation.

When I got home, I went to talk to Mom. "Why is my name Clara Louise?" I asked. "Mrs. Juno wants to know." I wanted to know, too!

> Time-order words and phrases show the order of events.

"You are named for your grandparents on Dad's side," said Mom. I was confused. My grandma's name was Carla. My grandpa's name was Lou.

> Dialogue between characters helps to move the story along.

Mom saw my puzzled face. "Well, I never really liked the name Carla," she chuckled. "I took the letters and mixed them up, and it came out Clara. Louise seemed like a girly version of Lou, so there you are."

> Exact words describe feelings, thoughts, and actions.

Now I knew! I was named for my grandparents, sort of. I had a good story to tell Mrs. Juno in school the next day.

> The story ending gives a sense of closure.

These generic scoring rubrics can be used in the evaluation of many types of written responses.

2-Point Rubric

2 Points	A 2-point response is accurate and complete, and fulfills all the requirements of the task. Necessary support and/or examples are included, and the information given is clearly text-based. Any extensions beyond the text are relevant to the task.
1 Point	A 1-point response includes some correct information, but may be too general or overly specific. Some of the support and/or examples may be incomplete or omitted.
0 Points	A 0-point response is inaccurate, confused, and/or irrelevant, or the student failed to respond to the task.

4-Point Rubric

4 Points	A 4-point response demonstrates an understanding of the task, completes all requirements, and provides an insightful or creative response to the prompt. Language and organization are sophisticated. Few or no errors in grammar or mechanics exist.
3 Points	A 3-point response demonstrates an understanding of the task, completes all requirements, and provides an adequate and comprehensive response to the prompt. Language is appropriate, and organization is logical. Few errors in grammar and mechanics exist, and those do not interfere with meaning.
2 Points	A 2-point response demonstrates a partial understanding of the task, completes some of the requirements, and provides an unfinished, inconsistent, or otherwise flawed response to the prompt. Language is simplistic, and organization may be hard to follow. Errors in grammar and mechanics exist.
1 Point	A 1-point response demonstrates minimal understanding of the task, fails to complete all requirements, and only tangentially refers to the prompt. Language is simplistic or inappropriate, and organization is illogical. Multiple errors in grammar and mechanics interfere with meaning.
0 Points	A 0-point response is irrelevant, illegible, incomprehensible, or not in English.